FROM SYLHET TO SHILLONG

Lala B.K. Dey with a forest officer.

FROM SYLHET TO SHILLONG

The Story of the Last IGP of Undivided Assam

A Biography

BIJOYA SAWIAN

SPEAKING TIGER

SPEAKING TIGER BOOKS LLP
125A, Ground Floor, Shahpur Jat, near Asiad Village,
New Delhi 110049

First published as *Unfolding the Legend: the Extraordinary Life of Lala B.K. Dey* 2020
First published by Speaking Tiger Books in paperback in 2023

ISBN: 978-93-5447-610-5
eISBN: 978-93-5447-612-9

10 9 8 7 6 5 4 3 2

Typeset in Crimson Roman by SÜRYA, New Delhi
Printed at Chaman Enterprises, New Delhi

Dedicated to
All those who are scattered and displaced
for reasons known and unknown

CONTENTS

Praise for the Book

I have just finished reading about the fascinating life of Lala B.K. Dey, the last IG of undivided Assam and a legend in himself. I was in college with his son, Bijon Dey, who himself reached the highest echelons of power as an IPS officer. The author of this book, Bijoya, is married to Alark Singh, with whom I studied in the same batch at Welham Boys, Mayo and St. Stephen's.

Lala B.K. Dey is a legend in the Assam Police, and I heard many stories of his exploits when I spent two years on deputation with the Meghalaya Police in the latter half of the 1990s. Some of these are detailed in this book. The Northeast has had a very turbulent history, especially during the period B.K. Dey was the IG, and yet he spent 8 years as the top cop in this region.

While I did not know him personally, I have worked under two of the finest IPS officers who were trained by him: Mr D.N.S. Srivastava and Mr P.C. Sharma, who was one of my predecessors as Director CBI. Mr K.P.S. Gill, who needs no introduction and was one of the finest IPS officers, was also trained by him.

To any reader who is interested in the history and culture of the Northeast, this book is a must read. My congratulations to Bijoya for putting it all together and paying a fitting tribute to a legendary police officer.

A.P. SINGH

Former Director, CBI
Member, UPSC

***

Bijoya Sawian deftly weaves the story of a young boy from Sylhet, who grows up to join the British Army in the Second World War, and finally retires as the last Inspector General of Undivided Assam. The narrative weaves in the twist and turns of colonial and post colonial worlds Lala B.K. Dey straddled, capturing historical events that one only reads of in coffee table books. That the book is written by his daughter decades after his death is not an easy task to endeavor—not to deify him but to keep him as human and as close to the man she remembers. As a memory keeper, she has excelled to touch spaces hitherto unknown and lost in the sands of time with warmth and sensitivity

MADHU GURUNG

Award winning author of *The Keeper of Memories* and *Tibet with My Eyes Closed*

***

Legends are called so because they leave a mark on peoples' minds long after they are gone. They are examples we can model our lives on because they have diligently followed their moral compass in their lifetime. One such legend is Lala Bimalendu Kumar Dey, who served as a police officer in undivided Assam and retired in 1978 as Director General of Police in Shillong.

PATRICIA MUKHIM

Editor, *Shillong Times*

***

I was gifted a copy of the book *Unfolding the Legend* by Smt. Bijoya Sawian, who I have known for years now through our mutual interests in indigenous culture and traditions of the Northeast.

This book chronicles the life and times of Lala Bimalendu Kumar Dey, who served as an Indian Police Service officer in undivided Assam. To me, it was striking to see the parallels between his and my own father's life, Late Lakheswar Barthakur, who passed away while serving as the first Director of Agriculture in undivided Assam in the pre-independence era. This made the book very real and personal for me as I was reading it.

The vivid descriptions of Lala Dey's life struggles and the success he attained through sheer determination, perseverance and hard work are an inspiration for every young man and woman. Legends are not born, they are made, and they live on in people's memories for their work and the principles they epitomized. Lala Dey is truly a legend—a first amongst equals.

Bijoya, through this book, has truly captured the nuances and multifarious character of her father. Through her distinct narrative, the author has brought to life and has managed to preserve the life and times of not only her father but a way of life that is to be celebrated and remembered.

(DR) DIPOK KUMAR BARTHAKUR
Former Vice-Chairman, State Innovation and Transformation Aayog, Assam
Former Chairman, Vivekananda Institute of Culture, Guwahati

***

Bijoya Sawian's heart-warming book on her father, late Lala B.K. Dey, the last IG Police of undivided Assam, a stalwart among men, is written in her signature style: lucid prose with meaningful reminiscences of an epic journey of a remarkable migrant family.

It charts the life of her father and his forefathers. This volume is truly a treasure trove of anecdotal delight with the narrative spanning the social and political history of the area in the nineteenth and twentieth centuries including World War II and the Partition of India.

SUDIPTA BHATTACHARJEE
Adjunct Professor of Media Science & Journalism, Brainware University Kolkata
Former Resident Editor (Northeast), *The Telegraph*

***

Praise for the Book

Bijoya Sawian's book on her father is a gripping account about the life and times of a doyen with a fascinating lineage and legacy. It is also a delightful read, both for historians and lovers of literature, about a far-flung and little-known part of our country, the 'enchanted frontiers'.

AJAY BAHADUR SINGH
(Sirmaur)

Foreword

A few days back, my son, Baluk, had called me in the afternoon to say that B.K. Dey Sawian, or Bijon as I know him, wanted to see me on a personal matter. In spite of the rapid spread of the pandemic, I could not say 'No'. I had known Bijon as a young Superintendent of Police when I was the Home Minister in the state, and later, when I was the Chief Minister of Meghalaya, he was my Police Chief.

And so we arranged to meet over a cup of tea at 11 am the following morning. I was rather looking forward to our meeting which would have given both of us the opportunity to recall our past association. It so happened that East Khasi Hills District including the capital city was put under lockdown and as a result, we had to speak over the telephone. Bijon told me that his sister, Bijoya Sawian, a well known writer and translator, was writing on the life and times of their father, Lala B.K. Dey, the last Inspector General of Undivided Assam, and she had conveyed a request that I write the Foreword for the book.

What an honour, I thought, to be made this request in my octogenarian years! I must admit that I have been very closely associated with the family for many decades. Mr Maham Singh, Lala B.K. Dey's brother-in-law, was my senior colleague in politics, both in the Cabinet and in the erstwhile Congress Party. Bah Benu, as we in Jaiaw know Lala Dey, was a member of our wider social group, having lived and grown up in the midst of a Khasi locality in Shillong. His parents had come up from Sylhet in the 1920s and had preferred to permanently settle down in our beautiful capital city.

His parents and brothers and sisters learnt the local language and spoke Khasi without a flaw. Two of the siblings, including Lala Dey, married into the community, and brought up the children in the typical matrilineal system. I, therefore, felt that I was duty-bound to pen my thoughts in this Foreword for the book.

Bah Benu is a personality who is known all over this remote region of our country not only because of his achievements in the police service but as a man with a human face—very unlike the policemen of his generation. And we, particularly the Khasis, felt proud of the fact that a man from our midst has had such an illustrious life and had attained great heights in whatever field he strived to achieve. He was a person who had the opportunity to have firsthand experience of the different historical events in the last century—the period under the British Raj, the Second World War, India's Independence and the immediate aftermath, and the different stages of demands for self-determination by the tribal communities of Northeast India and their subsequent achievements thereof.

On behalf of the author, Bijon had generally discussed the text of the manuscript with me. I must admit that the book will be a readers' delight. The details and information that have been incorporated in the chapters will be of immense use to historians and researchers who have an interest in the socio-political and economic life of the people of our region.

My greetings and best wishes to all in these very trying times that we are currently faced with.

D.D. LAPANG

Former Chief Minister of Meghalaya

Glossary

Bah: Respectful reference/appendage to a male elder

Kha: Paternal Aunt

Khasi: A tribal community inhabiting the Khasi Hills of the Indian state of Meghalaya. Also, the language spoken by this community.

Khohs: Conical shaped baskets. In this book, an ancient mode for carrying a person by porters.

Kong: Respectful reference/appendage to a lady

Kwai: Betel nut, commonly used with a combination of a herbal leaf (tympew) and lime to make a 'paan'. Referred to in the rest of India as supari.

Mama: Maternal Uncle

Mei: Mother

Meikha: Paternal Grandmother

Meirad/Rad: Maternal Grandmother

Meisan/San: Mother's Elder Sister/Female Cousin

Mithai: Sweets

Pakhynnah: Father's younger brother or his male cousin

Papa/Pa: Father

Parad: Maternal and Paternal Grandfather

Pasan: Father's elder brother/Elder maternal aunt's husband

Pu: A Mizo term for a male elder

Razakars: A rag-a-tag armed force under the Pakistan Army

SP: Superintendent of Police

Syiem: Literal meaning is Ruler but also used as surname by members of the ruling clans.

Prologue

This is the story of a man who held Duty above all else. Duty to the country, the people—regardless of class, colour, caste and creed; to the family—which included not only his parents, wife and children but his siblings, nieces and nephews on both sides of the family and to the helpless and needy. He was the one who loved to ride either alone or with like-minded companions deep into the silent forests, where he restored his clarity and composure, thus gaining wisdom and strength from the abundance of the natural world and the voice of his own conscience. He rode in the sunshine and in the storm with equal ease.

From Sylhet to Shillong, he bore the journey and life's challenges and excitement with true grit and gratitude. He embraced all the new cultures and presences as only he could.

He was my father, Lala Bimalendu Kumar Dey.

This is his story.

1

A Proud Son of Sylhet

My brother, Bijon, remembers:

'Lala Dey does not speak Bengali,' was what the Police Chief of West Bengal had to say about my father. It was an evening in Calcutta when my young wife and I had been invited over for tea to the residence of the Inspector General of Police. I did attempt to clarify that my father did speak what I believed was Bengali. Mr Ranjit Gupta, however, had made his point, and in those days, a three-pipper did not have the liberty to argue. We had a very pleasant and delightful evening with him and his elegant wife, Mrs Mina Gupta. I was then a sub-divisional police officer of a subdivision in the Midnapur District of West Bengal.

Months later, when we had come home on vacation for the naming ceremony of my firstborn, I told father what his friend and colleague had to say about him. I quoted the statement of Mr Ranjit Gupta verbatim and pat came the reply, 'I do speak Bengali when necessary but Sylheti is my mother tongue.'

***

Father was a linguist and had the gift of speaking several languages in perfect tone and accent. He spoke Gorkhali like a Gorkha, Assamese like the best in Assam, Hindi like someone from the North and when he spoke Khasi, he spoke like he was a native of Cherrapunjee. His English was perfect; he spoke the Queen's English. But it was something else when he spoke Sylheti. We would listen spellbound when a relative dropped by. 'There they go grinding their teeth!' a Sylheti cousin once said good-humouredly, knowing full well it was a very special moment not to be disturbed.

My father was 27 years of age in the year 1947. There were two events that occurred in that year that pained him immensely amidst the celebrations of our Independence. One was Partition itself and the other was Sylhet District's merger with Pakistan.

He was a man who felt deeply about his roots and was proud to be a Sylheti against all odds. Deep in his subconscious, he strongly believed in the community that he came from, and at the same time, he held all communities in great respect. In spite of the displacement of Partition, he kept in constant contact with his people in Sylhet and Sunamgunj and would render whatever help and assistance to them, whenever it was necessary, regardless of caste and creed. He never shied away when they called for help and they, in turn, firmly believed that he would not let them down.

His niece, Joyeeta Banerji, my aunt, Mira Ghosh's eldest daughter, summed up the 'family man' in my father beautifully. She wrote to me, 'I am so glad that you are writing about our redoubtable Boro Mama. His larger-than-life personality dominated any place he happened to be in. A devoted son, I remember what good care he took of his parents till their last days. He was a caring brother to his siblings and an affectionate uncle to his numerous nieces and nephews. He found time for each and every one of us despite his career and family responsibilities. We were so lucky to have him in our lives.'

These sentiments are echoed by many others in his family—cousins, nieces and nephews, now scattered all over the world. I can also confidently share the same opinion of him on behalf of all the family members of my mother.

On my last visit to Uncle Ataur Rahman, who was ailing and who was my father's colleague and friend, he said to me, 'There will never be another one like him. He was a great human being—kind, fearless, noble. He was proud of his roots and confident of himself.'

'He was a gentleman and a true aristocrat,' muses Mrs Jyoti Jafa, when she talked about her Shillong days where her husband Mr V.S. Jafa, a brilliant IAS officer, served in Assam and Meghalaya for many years.

His staff, those who served with him and who are still alive, say they still dream of him whenever in trouble and gain solace from that. Their tributes are part of this book.

Papa was a multi-faceted man who touched people's lives, leaving an indelible mark behind.

Lala Prasanna Kumar Dey
(1837—1921)

Lala Bijoy Kumar Dey
(1891—1975)

Lala Bimalendu Kumar Dey
(1920—2001)

2

A Bloodline of Courage and Perseverance

Srihalata and Shilhot, the original names of Sylhet, mean the 'Market of Stones'. The shilla stones abound in this area and have many uses, including as weapons to attack and deter the enemy. King Govind Gour, who ruled Sylhet in the late twelfth century, used them to protect his palace. The splendor of Sylhet is enhanced by emerald hills and sparkling water bodies stretching out languidly to the states of Tripura, Assam and the rest of East Bengal. The Indo–Bangladesh border is the longest land border in the world. The Indian states of West Bengal, Assam, Meghalaya, Tripura and Mizoram cradle the landmass of Bangladesh, letting a southern passage through which the journeying rivers flow onwards to the Bay of Bengal. The beels, the oxbow lakes formed by the tectonic subsidence during the earthquake of 1762 and the saucer-shaped water bodies, haors, add to the beauty of the Surma Valley, where Sylhet town, replete with history, sits with pride and beauty.

Days before the Great Shillong Earthquake of 12th June 1897, which shook the region and left a trail of devastation, my great-grandfather, Lala Prasanna Kumar Dey, a towering figure in Sylhet and Sunamgunj, also a renowned poet, captured the picturesque beauty of the Khasi Hills in one of his most beautiful verses. As he sat in his verandah in Sunamgunj one evening at sunset, watching the Surma valley sparkling with the water bodies and the distant hills silhouetted against the sky, he wrote these lines in a poem which he titled, 'A Fine Evening in June':

> 'A beauty then Sunamgunj wore,
> As ne'er it did before;
> I walked to the south most road
> To thus enjoy it more;
> And gazed around enchanted quiet
> A fairyland it seemed;
> The haor, river, hills and skies
> With charms transcendent gleamed;
> The Dekar haor's vast expanse
> A glitter unwonted showed;
> As kissed by evening's crimson rays,
> The wavelets count'nance glowed;
> The Surma grown to youth's full bloom,
> Impatient, seaward goes;
> What a girl of sixteen looks so brave,
> As first to her lover drawn;

The Khasi Hills a little off
In velvet green and bright;
And pagree-white how grand they look
In the sun's retiring light;
The castles in the West and East
All pendants in the air;
What human art can engineer
A masonry so rare.'

There was something prophetic in these words. It was as if he could see his family's future and destiny. It was up these hills, these 'castles ...pendant in the air,' that his eldest son, my grandfather, Lala Bijoy Kumar Dey, and his family would, one day, traverse to settle in another land.

It is also a marvelous coincidence because even now as I write, I remember my younger brother, Prabhat, and his wife, Partei, telling us of a picnic on the hills below Cherrapunji. The spot they chanced upon completely mesmerized them and made them dream of building a second home. They were totally unaware that the hill overlooked Sunamgunj.

Lala Prasanna Kumar Dey's collection of poems, *Indian Bouquet*, which he dedicated to Babu Nistaran Banerjee, an eminent Judge, was a much-lauded literary work. His poems have been included in the collection, *The Mapping of India: An Anthology of Indian Poetry in English, 1870-1920.* He was a student at the Hindu College, Calcutta (now known as the Presidency College) where he did his post-graduation in English and befriended many literary luminaries, among them Bankim Chandra Chattopadhyay. The shock and grief that he felt when the poet suddenly passed away at age fifty-five is expressed in a moving poem, 'Is Bankim Dead?'. He also wrote poems on Swami Vivekananda, Pandit Ishwar Chandra Vidya Sagar, Sures Chandra Biswas and Mona Mohan Ghosh among many others.

Calcutta was then known as the second city of the British Empire and throbbing with the pulse of the Bengal Renaissance. It was a time of the awakening of modern liberal thinking in nineteenth century Bengal. Great-grandfather Prasanna reveled in this atmosphere, being an intellectual and a thinker.

Unfortunately, while he was away in Calcutta, his father, Pran Krishnanath, lost most of his landed properties in Kajalsha and other parts of Sylhet due to the Sunset Laws. This unfortunate turn of events was brought about by the betrayal of his manager who did not deposit the land revenue before sunset on the appointed day. The manager connived to later purchase the estate himself at the auction. The story goes that the manager slowly lost his entire family, and distraught, he went to Lala Prasanna, confessed his misdeeds and was forgiven. By then, Lala Prasanna had settled down in Sunamgunj with his wife, Mohini Devi, and his three children—my grandfather Bijoy Kumar, his brother Hemant Kumar and his daughter Sailabala. He had started a new life, albeit a simpler one, doing service to the poor, writing poetry and also getting involved in the nationalist movement. It was around this time that he also decided to adopt the surname Dey and dropped Ray Chaudhury. He wanted a fresh new beginning without the burden of a tumultuous past for himself and his descendants. He also added the prefix Lala to enable the family to, immediately, connect with each other wherever they are. In Bengal there is no other family which has this title. It is presumed that he derived it from a scholar he admired, Lala Harkishen Lal, who taught Persian in the court of Murshid Kuli Khan (Subadar of Bengal 1717-1727).

Besides his love and talent for poetry, Lala Prasanna was a philanthropist and an educationist who believed in the importance of learning and knowledge for one and all. He felt deeply for the underprivileged who were denied this asset and established the first primary school in Sunamgunj, known as the Jubilee School, in 1877. He soon added a secondary section and the school was one of the important landmarks of progress in the district. It is now known as the Government Jubilee High School and has an impressive Alumni, among them the philosopher Dewan Mohammad Ajrof and former Bangladesh Foreign Minister Abdus Samad Asad. He also set up the Jubilee Press soon after. The Lala Bazaar and Lala Jheel in Sylhet were named after Lala Prasanna to commemorate his valuable contribution to Sunamgunj.

Lala Prasanna was a great friend of Sir Henry John Stedham Cotton who was a member of the Indian Civil Service (ICS) since 1867. Cotton was sympathetic towards nationalism and befriended many Indian people and families. My great-grandfather was one of them. He would often ask Lala Prasanna for advice in administration and governance during his various postings in Assam and Bengal, and Lala

Prasanna would be invited to meetings and all the ceremonial occasions. When he became the Chief Commissioner of Assam (1896-1902), a reception was held in his honour at Sunamgunj by the administration to which Lala Prasanna was invited. When great-grandfather was informed that there was a dress code and every one had to don a Western suit, he politely declined the invitation. When Sir Henry Cotton heard this and was told the reason, he sent a message that Lala Prasanna Kumar Dey can attend in his traditional attire. To the astonishment of all those gathered there, great-grandfather arrived in a white silk dhoti-kurta ensemble with an embroidered shawl draped elegantly around his shoulders. Sir Henry Cotton beamed with delight and apparently remarked, 'Here he comes, the grand old man!'

This story is reminiscent of one communicated to me by Naba Bhattacharjee who lives in Shillong. In the 1950s, his father was informed, before an event at the Shillong Club, that he was not to come in dhoti kurta but in a suit. He was very uncomfortable at the thought and confided in my father who was then the Deputy General of Police in Shillong. My father immediately wrote to the Secretary of the Club that this was an affront to a citizen of India and that apologies should be sent to him along with a fresh invitation and that Mr Bhattacharjee will attend in a dhoti kurta. The request was approved.

At the time of Sir Henry Cotton's departure for England in 1902, Lala Prasanna had subtly highlighted all his good deeds in a poem which he called 'Verses addressed to The

Honourable H.J.S. Cotton, Chief Commissioner of Assam, on the eve of his departure from India' (Appendix A).

Sir Henry Cotton

Tragedy struck Lala Prasanna's life when his young wife Mohini Devi suddenly passed away, leaving three young children. He was shocked and shattered and wrote,

> Say good doctor, say what's this?
> Why so looks my dear?
> Why this pallor o'er her face?
> Why this flow of tear?
> Speak a word my dearest wife
> Once more look at me
> What's this, what's this doctor dear?
> What, alas, I see?

Later, he married Heeramoyee Devi, who embraced the three young children as her own and also bore him six sons. His youngest son, Lala Naval Kumar De was born when great-grandfather was 82 years old. He was the same age as my father and they were great friends. Lala Naval Kumar De, or Nava kaka as he was known, was a fine gentleman and had a successful career as an officer in the Indian Army during the Second World War and later in the Indian Administrative Service of the Union Territories Cadre. His eldest daughter, Vaijayanti, and I were in the same class at Loreto Convent

Lala Naval Kumar Dey

Shillong, and we are in touch and friends to date. His eldest son, Lala Shyamol Dey, is one of the relatives who did meticulous research on the family history and published it in a paper titled 'Heera's Legacy'.

The family was settled in Murshidabad where, according to Papa, 'we served as naib subedars and subedars in the court of Siraj ud-Daulah.' One of the close relatives was the renowned Mohan Lal who was the last Dewan of Bengal, Bihar and Orissa in the court of the nawab and was the nawab's friend and confidant. After the Battle of Plassey in June 1757, the entire family fled to Purnea and other parts of Bengal, mostly across the Padma and into the remote lands of East Bengal. Later, the family settled down in Sylhet. They adopted the Sylheti language and customs and, through marriage, formed strong links with the landed families and contributed to the educational and cultural life of the place.

When we were young, all of us—my siblings and cousins—never went beyond the references to great-grandfather, Lala Prasanna, his father, Pran Krishnanath Ray and his grandfather, Jugal Kishore Ray Chaudhury because they were the only ones mentioned to us. Many of our generation also remember being told of a relative, Dewan Mohan

Lal and the 'great battle' which forced the family to flee from Murshidabad. In adulthood, some of my siblings and cousins, individually and unbeknown to each other, began researching the family tree intrigued by the many stories they heard as children. Based on their cumulative research which included going through land papers and other documents in Bangladesh, there emerged the possibility that we are descendants of Siraj ud-Daulah (Nawab of Bengal, Bihar and Orissa) from his consort, Begum Aleya, a further confirmation of the Murshidabad connection. Aleya was Mohan Lal's sister, Madhabi, also known as Heera for her great beauty. The name Aleya was given to her after her 'nikkah'.

My father never talked of the Siraj connection to us. Even in formal pujas, he did not go beyond five generations i.e. Jugal Kishore Ray Chaudhury. Is it the trauma of post-independence violence, based on religion, when the country was severed like a heart cut into two? Or is it that there were no official records of Siraj's son since the British destroyed all that was not convenient to them including mention of Mohan Lal? And Papa, being a stickler when it comes to facts and figures and to the written word, would prefer to restrict himself to those forefathers whose descent to him is incontrovertible. It is a mystery and we find it intriguing and as my father's eldest grandson, Atiar Dey, puts it, 'I think at some point in life we all want to know who we are and where we come from. We are happy that the topic has entered the academic arena.'

In 2012, a surprise did leap in from the academic world.

Professor Amalendu De, who had served as President and General Secretary of the Asiatic Society and who was also an eminent professor of Jadavpur University, concluded in his book in Bangla, *Sirajer Putro O Bangshadharder Sandhane,* that our family was, indeed, descended from Nawab Siraj ud-Daulah and Aleya. He found Aleya's grave in the famous cemetery Khosbagh in Murshidabad alongside Siraj ud-Daulah and Alivardi Khan during his visit as part of his research. In 2015, the book, which became an instant hit and best seller in West Bengal, Bangladesh and among all Bangla-speaking people around the world, was translated into English by Professor Nandini Guha under the name *In Search of Siraj's Son and Descendants*. The book draws our lineage from the six-year-old son of Nawab Siraj-ud-Daulah and Begum Aleya, who was rescued by Mohan Lal after the bloodbath of the Battle of Plassey, and later, adopted by a Hindu zamindar of Mymensingh in an elaborate ceremony in the presence of Mohan Lal. He was named Jugal Kishore Ray Choudhary. Mohan Lal, contrary to the inference of some historians, did not die in Plassey. According to the Yadav narrative, he continued to fight against the British, in disguise, and eventually settled in Guptipara where he passed away. A memorial stone was erected in his honour which exists to this day.

For many of us in the family, the ambiguity of our ancestry was laid to rest. For the others, devout and staunch Hindus for three centuries now, it was a discomfiting and incredulous revelation and they are, till now, firm in their belief that Mohan Lal was the main link to Murshidabad. I was brought up in a secular and all-embracing atmosphere so the possibility that five generations back, from my paternal side, my ancestor belonged to another faith and another land left me unperturbed. I simply remained as I was brought up—a child of mixed parentage—half Khasi, half Sylheti, who grew up in Shillong strictly in the Khasi tradition and culture, while at the same time respecting all cultures and denominations, just as my parents wanted it to be.

When I read the book, however, so many memories came flooding back to me. Of grandfather, Lala Bijoy Kumar Dey's book shelves with a sizeable collection of Persian and Arabic books along with his Law books, novels in Bengali and French and Russian classics. Of a morning long ago when I was told that my father would like me to join him in the verandah. Nothing strange about that but I was certainly surprised to find father with two men sitting with bundles of sarees spread on a thick sheet. Without much ado, Papa told me to choose some sarees for my sister, Parvati and myself. Before I could actually do so, he boomed, 'This will suit you Bibi and this is perfect for Parvati.' The two men without looking up even once handed the sarees over to me. Papa nodded and smiled as he proceeded to buy at least a dozen more which he later gave away as gifts. I went to my mother. I was intrigued. Father sitting patiently in the morning sun and buying sarees! Mei smiled, 'They are silks sarees from Murshidabad… very good silk,' she said. I stared at her and seeing me puzzled, she added, 'Murshidabad is famous for silk. The sariwalla is from there—where your father's family originally came from.' In bits of conversation with my aunts, they mentioned about the family fighting in a famous battle and, according to them, 'if it was not for treachery in the family, the family would still be in Murshidabad and the British would not have entered India.' Unfortunately, not once did I ask them to elaborate.

But let all that remain in the realms of literature and history because my father, as I mentioned earlier, did not talk of this part of his ancestry in detail, at least not to me and my siblings. Papa, who was a great rider, would always talk of General Mohan Lal with whom he shared the undying love for horses and the sport, and his grandfather, Lala Prasanna, the poet and dreamer whose photograph hung in the hall of our Mawprem home. It now adorns my brother Bijon's drawing room in his beautiful, pine-scented home in Annesville.

And this book is about Papa.

My grandfather, Lala Bijoy Kumar Dey, graduated from Cotton College Guwahati which was set up in 1901 and was named after Sir Henry Cotton, Chief Commissioner of Assam, and he obtained his Law Degree from Dacca University. He was married to Sulata Chaudhuri. My beautiful Meikha was one of the eight daughters of Jai Narayan Deb Chaudhuri, a prominent member of the landed aristocracy of Sylhet. Three of their seven children were born in Sylhet, with my father being the eldest. When Great-grandfather lost his landed properties, it became imperative for his son, Lala Bijoy, to seek new pastures and start a new life as a professional.

Knowing my grandfather, I am sure the prospect filled him with enthusiasm and excitement, albeit tinged with sadness.

As a brilliant lawyer with courage and determination, it was no issue for him to resettle in a strange land up in the hills. So in the spring of 1927, the family packed up and left for Shillong, which by then had become a well-established headquarters of the Province of Assam with the necessary trappings of a District and Provincial Court.

Father in St. Edmund's school uniform (extreme right) with his parents and siblings, Bina and Chitswarupanand, in Shillong (1928)

3

Up the Slopes Onto Unknown Pastures

In 1874, forty years after the British had subdued a strong resistance and guerilla war waged against them by the Khasi Raja U Syiem Tirot Sing, because the British reneged on their promise of giving him control of the passes to Assam if he gave permission for a railway through his land, the Northeast Frontier was made a separate province. The Chief Commissioner of the province of Assam was made directly responsible to the Governor General. In September of that year, Sylhet was separated from Bengal and was incorporated in the newly created province. This was done in order to facilitate and enhance the commercial development of the frontier province of Assam and consequentially the Assam-Sylhet railway was established in 1912. For many of the inhabitants of Sylhet, however, it was a sad and traumatic severance.

When Rabindranath Tagore visited Sylhet in the 1930s, he perhaps realized this and wrote an untitled poem on Sylhet which was later published under the title 'Sribhumi'. Grandfather Lala Prasanna had the privilege of meeting him at his best friend Rai Bahadur Nagendranath Chaudhuri's soiree at Khajanchibari. Tagore presented him with a signed copy of one of his books. Sadly, this precious gift is not traceable.

In the cruel stream of time
O land of beauty
Your heart is bound
with the heart of Bengal
with the garland of language
the blessings of Bengal are knotted
in the bond forever with you

In the early 1920s, organizations such as the Sylhet People's Association and Sylhet Bengal Re Union League mobilized public opinion demanding the division's incorporation into Bengal. During the Surma Valley Conference in 1928, however, leaders including Muhammad Bakht Mazumdar and Syed Abdul Majid opposed the transfer of Sylhet and Cachar to Bengal. Due to the size of the Bengali Muslim majority, the All India Muslim League formed the first elected government of Assam under the Crown.

So one year before the formation of the elected government, my grandfather brought his family up to settle in Shillong, the headquarters of British administration in the province of Assam, which included the Naga and Lushai Hills.

My aunt, Kha Bina (Sen) remembered feeling sad when they left the place where she spent most of her childhood, her maternal grandfather Jai Narayan Deb Chaudhuri's residence at Kastoghar in Sylhet. Vivid images of her home would come in waves every now and again. The front room was for visitors with an ante room attached to it which served as an office and where every morning, rice and lentils would be doled out to the needy. Next to it was the study where students from poor families were given basic education. On the other side of these two rooms was the large drawing room where the men met their friends in the mornings and evenings. The corridor that ran down the middle led to the courtyard where the two kitchens were situated at the end adjoining the separate wings for the men and women on opposite sides. The courtyard then opened out to an orchard

The track from Cherrapunji to Shillong.
People being carried by porters in cane khohs.

with a pond and patches of vegetables, the cow sheds and the staff quarters, the beautiful temple painted white and terracotta red. During the Civil War of 1970-71, the Razakars had burnt down the main house, leaving only the front façade intact so as to ward off attention and adverse publicity.

Papa talked of the journey up as if he was relating a story, his tone laced with nostalgia. He remembered his uncle, Jnanendra Narayan Deb Chaudhuri (Montu Mama) and him being carried by porters in khohs, which are conical shaped cane baskets, up the slopes, the topography changing as they moved away and higher. He noticed the trees and the betel nut and orange plantations. He remembered the excited chatter between the two of them as they watched the shimmering waters of the Surma receding before them. They passed villages with lakes and bustling markets amidst fields of crops winding lanes and tracks, all new to the two wide-eyed youngsters. Whose lands are these, Papa asked the porter, whose markets and villages. Each time the answer would be 'Babu Sib Charan Roy.' Papa and Montu Mama wondered who this man was and when they heard that he resided in Shillong, they were sure they would meet him.

Father's brothers and Montu Mama

It is one of those marvelous coincidences in life for they did meet my granduncle, Sib Charan Roy, who became very fond of my father. In school, my father was Sib Charan Roy's nephew Maham Singh's best friend and later he married his niece, my mother, Lisimon Sawian. Montu Mama was uncle Maham's colleague as both were advocates in the Shillong Bar, so they too became friends and colleagues.

With Khasi friends and Uncle Maham

Papa said, as they climbed higher and higher, the air became fresh and crisp and had an alien fragrance. He noticed the trees were different and the bird songs too. While savouring this new experience, he watched Sylhet slowly receding into a blur. He asked Montu Mama how far Shillong was from Sylhet and Montu Mama replied that it was very far. My father retorted that it could not be so far that he could not walk back if he wanted to. He said it with conviction, as Sylhet became just a dot, a bit of land and a bit of water—like an eye with a teardrop. Montu Mama was silent. They were both seven years old.

Then, all of a sudden, Sylhet was nowhere in sight.

Kha Bina had said to me one day, 'I think your Papa left a bit of himself in Sylhet.'

My grandparents in front of the Jaiaw House, with my three aunts, Bina, Mira and Mainu, and their first grandchild, Milonee.

Shillong lies on a plateau, the only major uplifted structure in the northern Indian shield. A pretty town, cradled by pine forests, it stands at an altitude of 5000 feet above sea level. Most Bengali families, who had moved to the Hills for trade or government jobs, chose to settle down in the predominantly non-Khasi Laban and Jail Road, but grandfather, Lala Bijoy Kumar Dey, decided to live in the heart of a patrician Khasi locality. He chose Jaiaw, a house which belonged to a Chinese family, which they later bought. It was a lovely tin roofed house built in the style that was adopted after the Great Earthquake with rose creepers on the walls and an archway covered with honeysuckle, framing the entrance at the gate.

My siblings and I would visit Meikha and Parad at least twice a month, and in accordance with Khasi tradition, would take fruits for them while Khasi sweet delicacies would be replaced with sweets from Delhi Mistan Bhandar, the best mithai shop in town. Fond memories are fresh in my mind of a bustling household full of chatter in Sylheti, English and in Khasi if neighbours had dropped by. If one closed one's eyes and listened to my aunts speak in Khasi, you would never have imagined that they were not Shillongites—so perfect was their tone and accent. Kong Sarahlin Tham, the younger daughter of Jor Manik Syiem of Mylliem, who lived close by, recollects Kha Bina's wedding and the reception in Dinam Hall, the family's 'pretty house and the members' perfect Sohra accent!' When I met my youngest uncle Pakhynnah Kalyan in New Delhi after four decades, I immediately noticed this too. After all, in our conversation a few sentences in Khasi were inevitable. He is now settled in the United States with his family. Till very recently, he had a summer home in Wales. He would drive around in his vintage motorbike all over the countryside which is so evocative of Shillong.

Meikha was a true epitome of her genteel background in her hospitality and grace. She was beautiful and shared her beauty secrets with me when I was barely in my teens (a quick face and hand massage with fresh cream before a bath) as I used to spend many mornings with her, just happy being around. She was always elegantly dressed in pastel shades. It was Taat and Tangail sarees in summer till spring and Murshidabadi and Benarasi silks in autumn right through the winter. She seldom wore jewelry except for her gold bala and a ruby ring. The Jaiaw house always had plenty of food, and at the drop of a hat, an impressive table would be laid. Ram Thakur the cook's mutton curry was a specialty, not to mention the array of vegetable and fish delicacies and the payesh, of course.

I have wonderful memories of celebrating one of my birthdays in Jaiaw along with my cousins, Milonee and Monica, who were so smart and fashionable. They had just returned from Belgrade where their father, Colonel Amar Sen, was the Military Attaché. Also present was Kha Mainu's pretty little daughter, Meenakshi.

My three gorgeous aunts, always so lively and warm, presented me with a powder blue silk dress with lace on the collar and sleeves, tightened at the waist and tied behind with a ribbon, and then flaring down to my knees in ripples. It was certainly the most elaborate and girlie dress I ever owned. In Umsohsun, my maternal grandmother's residence where we grew up, beiges, blues and whites were the preferred colours, though elaborately embroidered. Cottons and flannel in summer and autumn; maroon and light brown velvets in winter.

Most summers Jaiaw would burst into life when my other three lovely cousins from Calcutta—Joyeeta, Brinda and Esha would descend with colourful toys and exotic toffees all the way from Calcutta, in pretty flowery dresses. Sweaters from Hoondamal & Sons on the G.S. Road were popular welcome presents for them as the house would resonate with their incessant, cheerful chatter. To this day, I still share that rapport with all of them in many an enjoyable winter in Kolkata.

Meikha was very house-proud and related an incident when relatives, who wanted to settle down in Shillong, suddenly trooped in with bag and baggage. Her budget went awry and her plan to buy new curtains for the bedrooms seemed uncertain. She went to Parad, my grandfather, and expressed her disappointment. Apparently, he looked at her startled and boomed, 'Stick newspapers on the windows. Talking of curtains when people are seeking shelter?' Meikha, who was thirteen years younger, understood but wept copiously. Just as I did when I heard he wanted to destroy all the Coke ads in which I featured with my two college friends Manjit and Dimpy in the late 1960s. It was the first Coke ad in India and I was rather pleased with myself. I did not visit him for a year feigning illness each time.

My grandfather's practice picked up quickly and the family settled down comfortably. People talked of Parad's brilliance in court, his arresting looks, blazing eyes and superb voice and diction that would reverberate across the courtroom when he pleaded his cases. He was president of the Shillong Bar Association from 1958 to 1972, till he suffered a stroke and had to resign and also stopped his practice. He was also the founder of the first English weekly in Shillong in 1934. The Shillong Mail, a contemporary of the Rangoon Mail, was later revived by Shri Sudhindra Bhushan Choudhuri, a relative from Sylhet, and was renamed, The Shillong Times (An extract of an article by S.B. Choudhuri is in Appendix B).

The first thing that was done after they settled in Shillong, as would be expected from any family, was to find a good school for the children. My aunt Kha Bina joined the Jail Road Bengali Girls' High School and my father, being the eldest, was admitted to St. Edmund's College, where he learned under the Irish Brothers. His principal was Brother McCann.

Lala B.K. Dey (third row, second from right) at St. Edmund's School (1934)

St. Edmund's was established by the Congregation of Christian Brothers in Laitumkhrah, a cosmopolitan locality of Shillong, in 1916. The Brotherhood was founded by the Blessed Edmund Rice. The undergraduate section of the college was established in 1923. Brother J.E. McCann was the first principal of the school and college. At that point in time, the school was affiliated to the University of Cambridge in England and the undergraduate section was affiliated to the University of Calcutta. Papa wrote the Senior Cambridge Examination in 1936 and graduated with Honours in Economics from St. Edmund's College in 1941.

My father was an all-rounder. He was a brilliant student yet he had time for the outdoors, particularly horse riding. He would often go out on long treks on the numerous bridle paths astride the race horses which belonged to family friends. On one such outing, he and his horse had tumbled down the hillside when the horse lost its footing on the slippery track. The horse suffered minor cuts and bruises but father was riddled with wounds. He walked his ride to a nearby stream, and after washing up, he went home and covered himself with sufficient clothing to ward off the attention of his parents. It was only after a few days, when he developed mild fever that it came to be known that he had met with this riding accident. There was hell let loose. Grandfather gave him a 'rocket' while Meikha, who doted on her eldest son, nursed his cuts and wounds. This incident, however, did not deter him from his love and passion for horses.

Later, as a grandfather, he would ever so often load

up two horses in a truck and drive behind along with his grandson, Larsing, up to Diengiei, which in Khasi folklore is believed to be an extinct volcano. They would ride together all over the countryside and end the late afternoon with a canter to the hilltop from where they could see our family home at Mawprem, bathed in the receding sunlight.

In a certificate dated 28th November 1941, Brother J.I. O'Leary, the principal of St. Edmund's College, had written the following: 'Lala Bimalendu K. Dey was a student of this school and college for about twelve years. He graduated with Honours in Economics from this college in 1941.

'He had a uniformly bright career obtaining First Grade in the Senior Cambridge Examination 1936. He was a brilliant and witty speaker of the Debating Society, played most outdoor games well and was generally reliable...' (Appendix C).

Father with brothers-in-law, Maham Singh and Kynpham Singh, and my eldest aunt's husband, Pasan Hipshon Roy (1961)

Upon his graduation, my father was all set to leave for England to study law in one of the Inns of Court when the war broke out. He did the next best thing. He applied for a commission in the army—a decision he never regretted. In fact, he would remember his days in the army as some of the best years of his life, relating stories to us, usually after tea, his eyes softening in the fading light.

4

Into a Future of War and Peace

Officers Training School, Bangalore, September 1942. Seated centre the iconic Major (Later Lt General) Jagjit Singh Arora. Standing third row from left, Second Lieutenant L.B. Kumar Dey.

After graduating from the Officers Training School in Bangalore and on completion of the gunnery course at the School of Artillery, Deolali, father was commissioned into the 25 Mountain Regiment of the Royal Indian Artillery (now with Pakistan) in 1942. His first posting was Quetta. Papa's face would light up at certain memories and one of them was of his arrival in Quetta.

Quetta in Pashto means fortress. Surrounded by the Chittan, Takatu, Zanghoom and Murdaar mountains, it spreads below them as one of the most beautiful cities of Pakistan. It was winter when my father arrived. He told us that it was bitterly cold and the snowflakes were falling gently on his head like confetti. For a young man who grew up first in the balmy plains of the Surma Valley and, later, in the wooded rolling hills above it, the startling majesty of the landscape and the shower of snowflakes left an indelible mark, a memory he would cherish all his life. It was the beginning of five glorious years in the army where he made friends that lasted a lifetime. His admiration for English discipline, sense of duty above all else and, of course, the quintessential English humour became part of him.

From Quetta, Papa's unit was sent to Central India to engage in pre-war exercises with the 7 Indian Division. From there, his regiment was shipped to the Burmese Arakans where they inflicted the first major defeat of the Japanese Imperial Army in the 'Battle of the Boxes'. Subsequently, the unit was flown by air from the Arakans to stem the advance of the Japanese forces at the famous Battle of Kohima and Imphal.

Before the 161 Indian Brigade arrived from the Arakans, the only fighting troops in the Kohima area were the newly raised 1st Battalion of the Assam Regiment and a few platoons from the 3rd Battalion of the paramilitary Assam Rifles.

During the Second World War, India was under the British Raj. When war was declared in 1939, British occupied India also joined in as part of the Allied Nations. India sent over two and a half million soldiers to fight against the Axis powers comprising Germany, Italy and Japan. India also provided the base for American operations in support of China in the 'Burma India Theatre'. Kohima's strategic importance in the wider 1944 Japanese Chindwin offensive was its location at the summit of a pass that offered the Japanese the easiest route from Burma into India. The battle was often referred to as the 'Stalingrad of the East'. According to Wikipedia, in 2013, the British National Army Museum voted the Battle of Imphal and Kohima to be 'Britain's Greatest Battle'.

The Battle of Kohima was the turning point of the Japanese U-Go offensive into India in 1944. The battle, one of the bloodiest in history, raged for almost three months from 3rd April to 22nd June. In the first stage of the battle, the Japanese attempted to capture the Kohima ridge. This was important as it dominated the road by which supplies were being sent to the besieged British and Indian troops at Imphal. The British and Indian troops started their counter attack on April 18th to drive out the Japanese from the positions which they had occupied. This continued till May

13th. The Japanese retreated but continued to block the Kohima-Imphal Road. Then, from May 18th, the British and Indian reinforcements, including the 7 Indian Division which had been flown in from the Arakans, led a counter attack to retrieve the places which the Japanese had occupied and successfully reopened the road. The battle ended on 22nd June when the British and Indian troops in Kohima and Imphal met at Milestone 109 and ended the siege of Imphal. In this battle, Papa was commanding the guns which were positioned on a hilltop next to a church, when he lost his Forward Observation Officer and best friend Lieutenant J.S. Scott of the Royal Artillery who was out in the field. Later, when he became DIG in-charge of Naga Hills in 1957, he went looking for Jack's grave but could not find it…not then.

The Kohima War Cemetery sits on the ridge below the town, above the tennis court of the Deputy Commissioner's compound, where one of the fiercest encounters of the battle took place. A well manicured garden where roses bloom during season, it is one of the most visited places in Northeast India. At the two ends rise two tall structures with the Cross, and between them terraces climb up the slope. All along the terraces, there are stone markers embedded with bronze plaques carrying the name of each soldier who lost his life in this famous battle. These markers are made distinct with lime wash. There are two memorial crosses—one at the upper end and the other at the lower end of the cemetery. One commemorates the names of the Indian and Sikh soldiers. The epitaph inscribed on this memorial reads—'Here around the tennis court of the deputy commissioner, lie men who fought in the battle of Kohima in which they and their comrades finally halted the invasion of India by the forces of Japan in April 1944.' The lower-end memorial is dedicated to the 2nd British Division. It is a 15ft tall stone which had been brought from the spur in Maram, a traditional Naga burial stone. At the top of the memorial are the words on a bronze plate—'When you go home tell them of us and say for your tomorrow we gave our today.'

Interestingly, in a letter to my brother Bijon, a retired British Officer who had served with the 25 Mountain Regiment during World War II had written as follows, '...by the way it was troops of 7 Indian Division which recaptured the majority of the Jap strong points in Kohima more than the 2nd British Division (who got most of the publicity in this country—which is a shame).'

Bijon and my cousin Wallamphang recollect the day Lieutenant J.S. Scott's memorial plaque was located. It was the year 1968. They both accompanied my parents who visited the famous War Cemetery in Kohima. A posse of policemen were, as expected, in attendance too. Everyone was searching for Jack's grave. Mei, who by then had developed arthritis, was strolling quietly behind a very excited group led by my father, when she sighted some beautiful pink roses near a wall. Flowers, for Mei, were irresistible. To her, they were little gifts from heaven! She shuffled towards this glorious sight when she noticed a grave at her feet. On it was the name Lieutenant J.S. Scott. My father paid his respects and stood there for a long time—a mission of the heart completed. Bijon, who later thought it may have been a dream as the experience was so poignant and surreal, revisited it. When he took over as the Inspector General of the BSF Frontier, he sent his officers to go and locate the grave—a 'is it really there' kind of expedition. Yes, it was. So he too went and paid his respects to his father's friend lost in the war.

In 2004, Colonel John F. Kenyon OBE, MC, the President of the Shropshire Branch of the Burma Star Association wrote to Bijon, 'Jack Scott and I were also friends. I helped carry his coffin to the place of temporary repose—I could even show you where that was—perhaps near the Jessami track travelling east from Kohima. I would dearly love to have a copy of the photo you took of his permanent grave—WHAT A COINCIDENCE!' This loss, also meant the loss of a Military Cross for Papa as the death of an English officer under one's command was unforgivable. For my father, however, it would always be the death of a friend with whom he shared some unforgettable moments amidst a most horrific battle. The American historians, Allan Miller and Williamson Murray wrote, 'Nowhere in World War II did the combatants fight with more mindless savagery.' But it was inevitable, in my opinion; after all we had a ferocious enemy.

After the war, Papa languished for a while in the Rangoon Military Hospital struck by malaria and the 'Burma Dysentery'. It was a period of fatigue and introspection as the gunfire subsided and a strange silence pervaded the entire world which was struggling to reconstruct life after the war.

The only reading material that was available to him was the occasional newspaper that came to the Military Hospital. The other inmates received letters regularly from friends and relatives at home. Our family and, particularly my father's family, were not known for letter writing. This caught the attention of a young English nurse. It is believed that she had asked her friends to send postcards and letters of 'cheer' to my father and no sooner, piles of letters and postcards, addressed to Captain L.B. Kumar Dey arrived at the Rangoon Military Hospital. I do remember that cheerful pile of postcards, most of them from Croydon. Mei and I went through them with amusement and much gratitude. My father was obviously touched by the gesture of this young lady and they became good friends. He would often drive her around the ravaged city of Rangoon in his Ford Jeep. However, the day came when he had to bid her farewell as his unit had to board the troop ship for India.

One day, whilst in Rangoon, he came across an advertisement in a newspaper for the Commissioned Army Officers who wished to join the Indian Police and the Indian Civil Service. He opted for the police service as he felt that adjustment would be quite easy and natural, the police being a uniform service. It also carried with it the perquisite of a home posting. In the intervening period, the 3rd Field Regiment, to which Papa had been assigned at the end of hostilities in 1945 in Burma, was ordered to deal with internal disturbances in the North West Frontier.

On 27th April 1947, my father, who was then an Acting-

Major commanding the 35 Field Battery with Headquarters at Rawalpindi, was informed that he had been considered for his appointment in the new All India Police Service and on receiving an offer for transfer of service, he requested to be released from the army. (Copy of the offer Letter in Appendix D). It was on 30th June that year that father bade farewell to his colleagues and friends with a heavy heart, to face yet another challenge in his home province, Assam.

On his arrival at the provincial headquarters in mid-July 1947, he met with the last English Inspector General of Police of Assam, James Edward Reid and they immediately took to each other as Reid was also from the army. Many stories were shared at evenings at the IG's residence, one about how Reid lost a lung in the First World War. James Edward Reid asked Papa to command the Independence Day Parade in Gauhati on 15th August 1947. That was the beginning of his long and illustrious career as a policeman and his enduring love for Assam and the hills of the Northeast and its people.

PHOTOGRAPHS FROM FATHER'S WAR COLLECTION

(Left): School of Artillery Deolali (1942)
(Below): An Officer of the Royal Artillery in a Pathan Fort, Baluchistan (1943)

(Left): With colleagues and a guideat Taxila (April 1947)
(Right): In battle fatigues 'Ready for Kohima' Dimapur (1944)

(Left): At Dhond, with a colleague on their return from Burma (1945)
(Right): Memorial Monolith at the Kohima War Cemetery

(Above): Relaxing with officers during a joint exercise before 7 Indian Division's departure for the Burmese Arakans (1943)
(Right): Memorial plaque of Lieutenant J.S. Scott, Royal Artillery who died in Kohima (1944)

5

The Long and Arduous March

I would like to begin this chapter with a most endearing essay written by my youngest sister, Nayantara, when she was in Loreto Convent, Shillong. She was 8 years old.

'My father is in the government service in the Police Department. At present, he is the Head of the Department.

'It is an important department. Without it, there would be chaos, lawlessness and it would be unsafe to move around in lonely places. It is the police that track down murderers, thieves and looters, gangsters and other criminals. When we go anywhere and lose our way or get into trouble, we go to the police for help. The lower grades of policeman have to be on duty night and day, rainy or sunny even if there are festivals or holidays. A policeman will be seen everywhere.

'Isn't it a tiring job?'

Indeed it was, but it was also an important part of her father's eventful life.

Papa's career in the police was a long and colourful one. There were some periods which he would reminiscence with satisfaction and joy and some with sorrow and remorse. 'Sometimes, in the call of duty, one has to do things one does not want to, and then there are times when one also makes a mistake and at other times as the boss, one has to take responsibility for others' mistakes.'

Senior Officers of the Assam Police. My father is to the right of Mr B.K. Barua IGP, his predecessor. PTC Dergaon (1964)

L.B. Kumar Dey (age 48 years) in his office chamber as Inspector General of Police, Assam (1969)

He served as the Superintendent of Police of the United Khasi and Jaintia Hills, of Cachar, Kamrup and Sibsagar Districts before being promoted as the DIG in-charge of Naga Hills in 1957. He took the full-fledged command of the police force of composite Assam on 1st January 1969 and remained at the helm until November 1975.

In recognition of his distinguished career, he was appointed the Honorary Aide de Camp to four Presidents of India, Dr Zakir Hussain, Shri V.V. Giri, Shri Fakhruddin Ali Ahmed and Shri Neelam Sanjeeva Reddy. (Government of India's Notification may be seen in Appendix E).

Receiving Dr Zakir Hussain, President of India at Guwahati Airport as Governor B.K. Nehru looks on (April 1969)

His career as a policeman began most dramatically. Brigadier Amlan Pratap Datta VC recalled it in one of his articles, 'It was a chilly December night, an icy wind from beyond the mountains swept the plains. A motley crew of security men crept through the dense undergrowth of the foothills. The year was 1948. The Pakistan Army had moved in and occupied a huge tract—the Patharia Hill Reserve in the Cachar District. The Assam Police had dispatched a dashing young officer to reclaim the territory. Reinforced by troops from the Assam Regiment, under the command of Captain Lalmingliana Tochhawng, the officer and his men zeroed in on the enemy. The enemy ensconced in bunkers on the hills was taken by surprise. The 'brave hearts' pushed back the intruders after a fierce gun battle. For Lala B.K. Dey, the young officer who led the charge it was a moment of glory.'

'We drove away the intruders and re annexed the territory which thankfully is still a part of India to this day,' my father recalled later.

With police personnel in Silchar, front row on chair fourth from right (1948)

The Patharia Hills Reserve Operations was of great importance to the territorial integrity of NE India. If the Pakistani Army, backed by the Razakars had held their ground, the geography of this part of India would have been very different. The District of Sylhet had voted for its merger with Pakistan through a referendum. The Nagas had declared their Independence twelve hours before the midnight of 15th August. The Maharajas of Tripura and Manipur were vacillating on their accession to the Indian union. The resultant effect of Pakistan's occupation of the Patharia Hills would have led to the entire southern tract of Northeast India being excluded from the Indian Union. The District of Cachar which already had a sizeable Muslim population would have naturally merged with Pakistan and the Lushai Hills (now the Indian state of Mizoram) would have become part of the Chittagong Hill Tracts, leave alone the futures of Manipur and Tripura. It is for researchers and military historians to examine this aspect of history which has been totally ignored, which is the unfortunate narrative of the Northeast till today.

For this act of valour, father received the special appreciation of the government for maintaining the rights of the State of Assam in the Patharia Hills Reserve in January 1949 'in a distinctly hazardous situation' as was conveyed by the Inspector General of Police, Assam.

In the aftermath of Partition, streams of families, bag and baggage continued to cross over from East Pakistan to settle in the plains of Assam. The State and Central governments were very concerned as this influx would create an imbalance in the demography of the region. A group of officers were asked to look into this issue and recommend ways to contain the problem without causing human tragedy. My father, along with Mr B.C. Sarma of the IPS, Lt. Colonel S.S. Pandit, Lt. Colonel B.S. Bali and Lt. Colonel Chotu Singh Rathore laid the foundation and had set the traditions of a fine border guarding force in the 1st, 2nd and the 3rd Battalions of the Border Security Force under the Government of Assam. He was granted a Special Pay of Rs. 200 per month, no paltry sum in those days, for putting in place the idea that he had conceived in early 1950 when he was assigned the responsibilities for Border Security duties. (Copy of the government sanction of Special Pay in Appendix F.) The 3rd Battalion of this elite force, however, was redesignated as the 3rd Assam Police Battalion and it was sent to Naga Hills to deal with the armed uprising in the district. The State Government had then considered it incorrect to deploy an armed force against its own people.

I remember my father telling me that in 1965 after the Indo-Pak War, Mr K.F. Rustomji wanted to name the new raising of a Central Force as Border Force or BF in abbreviation, but father told him 'Sir, it is not a good idea. BF is short for bloody fools!' Mr Rustomji then consequently christened the new force as the Border Security Force, after the one in Assam. (L)Colonel Padam Singh Thapa, who was close to the officers involved in this historic formation and had met my father, commented 'Lala Dey was the inspiration and brain behind this force.'

I like the story of his meeting with the Naga rebel leaders and chieftains at the behest of the then Chief Minister of Assam Shri Bishnuram Medhi. Father was then DIG in-charge of Naga Hills and this time, thirteen years after the Battle of Kohima, he returned to Naga Hills on a different mission—reconciliation.

Nagaland is a mountainous state surrounded by the states of Arunachal, Manipur and Assam and Peoples 42 Republic of Myanmar to the East. There are twenty major tribes and sixty spoken dialects. People communicate with each other in broken Assamese which is referred to as Nagamese. The indigenous faith is a form of animism, nature worship and the presence of several deities and spirits. In mid-nineteenth century, 70% of the people converted to Christianity. When Independence was declared in 1947, the Nagas put up a referendum that they did not want to join the Indian Union. Nehru, infuriated, sent the army to suppress the rebellion but the problem was not solved. The struggle continues to this day.

'I remember the meeting had been arranged with the Naga chieftains, elders and the public and a stage had been set up. I did not think the stage was a good idea if I was to talk to them about peace and reconciliation. So my chair was brought down and I sat among them. I talked to them in Hindi and Assamese and told them the many advantages that they would reap if they stopped their rebellion against their country and joined the Indian Union peacefully. They listened very quietly and attentively, the chieftains, the heads of different groups who would soon become the most dreaded rebels, and the general public. As I kept hearing more murmurs of 'hmnhmn' and seeing their rapt attention and even some nods, I got more charged and my speech apparently lasted for over 45 minutes. When I finally ended, I told them to think for a while and let me know. I was sure it would be good news. It did not take long, however, for a Naga Elder to stand up and speak to me. He looked me in the eye and said 'Theek hai. Aap accha admi hai lekin hum log indipinkdink mangta' *Ok. You are a good man but we want 'indipinkdink'*. I was stunned. It was not good news but what was indipinkdink? I did not want to ask him as that would be an affront. Nagas are a proud people and if I did not understand, it was my fault. Then in a flash it struck me. He meant independence. They want independence. I thanked the man as I walked away, despondent of course but at the same time I did not feel I had lost anything. I felt privileged that I had such a close encounter with this magnificent tribe.'

He had a special feeling for them.

Sentila Yanger reminiscences about my parents' visit to her home in 1972, 'I remember your father's visit to our ancestral home in Mokokchung to see my grandfather, Marsosang Ao. He took time off from his official duties and came over with your mother and Nayantara. I was very young but I remember they all spent a warm and enjoyable time together. My grandfather and the family were so happy and honoured by the visit and presented your father with a shawl.'

With village headman and representatives in the Naga Hills (1957)

My father was not a person who believed that working from a 'desk' was the sine qua non of efficiency. He would tour the length and breadth of the state; as he would often say, 'The Police Chief is an inspecting agent of the government and, therefore, he has been designated as the Inspector General.' He was a man who was committed to being at the forefront of all situations. The inspiration and this attribute must have come to him from his years in the army when his regiment was a part of the Fourteenth Army under the command of then Lt. General & later Field Marshal Sir William Slim. Very interestingly, the Field Marshal had sarcastically observed in his book *Defeat into Victory* about the Supreme Headquarters and he had written, 'I found Supreme Headquarters a fascinating place to wander through. It was full of interesting people, not least persuasive young men interested in selling short cuts to victory, of which they held the rights of way. These 'racketeers' as I called them, were of two kinds, those whose acquaintance with war was confined to large non-fighting staffs where they had had time and opportunity to develop their theories, and tough, cheerful fellows who might be first-class, landed on a beach at night with orders to scupper a sentry-post, but whose experience was about the range of a tommy-gun.' (Extract from the book in Appendix G).

My father had the good fortune of having in Mr A.N. Kidwai of the Indian Civil Service, as the Chief Secretary of Assam. Mr Kidwai had an unprecedented tenure of ten years as the Chief Executive of the government when the region was going through its most difficult times—the Naga Rebellion, the language agitation, the Chinese aggression of 1962, the uprising in the Lushai Hills, the Indo-Pak war to name but a few. Unlike most Civil Servants, Mr Kidwai was an avid traveller. He and papa would traverse across the region to meet district officials, oversee development projects of the government at their specified location, and spend time with members of the civil society including the tea planters in the Brahmaputra and Barak valleys. The two were great friends and they enjoyed these journeys together.

Bijon also remembers the drive from Garo Hills through Goalpara along with the then Superintendent of Police of Garo Hills, Shri HK Bhattacharya. My father relied a great deal on Mr Bhattacharya's commendable ability to assess

Inspection—Connecting with His Men

situations and predict possible consequences. As they were approaching Mancachar, a border settlement, Uncle Hiranya told my father, 'Sir, you will see on the right-hand side the fields are filled with crops. Not an inch of space is left uncultivated. Now look to your left, there are more empty spaces than patches of cultivation. There will be a time when the people on the right will cross over to the left side of this road and these very patches will be filled with crops too every single inch.' The land on the right side of the road had settlers who had migrated from erstwhile East Bengal. On the left was the local population of tribals and non-tribals. My father was deeply saddened when the government, instead of taking heed of his assessment, took affront instead and Mr Bhattacharya had to face a trying and difficult time for many years.

Papa was known for his visits to distant police outposts in different parts of the state. He enjoyed the journeys and felt it was hugely important to connect with his officers and personnel in these far-flung places. During these visits, he would never fail to drop by at the Unit Welfare Centre, where the wives of police personnel were taught stitching and weaving and could, therefore, earn that extra penny to support the family. The police schools were topmost on his list of places to be visited, as he firmly believed that education was of utmost importance for all walks of life. There is a favourite story which my cousin Marphrang would relate of a visit in which he and my brother Prabhat accompanied Papa for a visit to the 'Naga trail' in the North Cachar Hills, along with other senior officers including the Deputy Inspector General of Police and the Commandant of the Armed Police Battalion. The whole outpost was ready and was called to a stand-to as Papa went around. Apparently, he suddenly stopped and narrowed his eyes towards a bunker and then, smiling, he strode towards it, shouting in his booming voice, 'Bendang Ao, kaise hai?' *Bendang Ao, how are you?* This was such a shock to the armed constable who had served as my father's orderly during his tenure in the Naga Hills that he dropped his light machine gun on the floor of the bunker and stood rooted to the ground. They met warmly as all those around looked on, stunned and deeply moved. Papa asked him after his family and so on and then patted him on the back and said, 'Shabaash.' That was one trait he had—he never forgot a face and a name and he enjoyed meeting the ones who had served with him, especially the often ignored and 'faceless minions.' To him, that was not what they were. They were special and he gave them full respect. Mr B.S. Baber, a former Director General of Police had written in one of his article, 'When I was DIG in the IGP's Office, his (Lala Dey's) advice was to see that the men are not starved and also to exercise all the powers of the IGP but keep him informed. He was a leader who could delegate the authority to his officers in the interest of the force.'

This great affection for those who served with him was a trait he shared with my mother. I remember being sent off with Kong Phris, my mother's maid and companion, from Guwahati via a night at Dergaon. We were to visit his driver Havildar Ram Bahadur in the Dibrugarh Hospital who my parents had met a week before. My mother told me that Ram Bahadur was dying of cancer, and he had expressed his wish to meet my brothers and sisters and cousins but since I was the only one present, I should go along with Kong Phris as he was keen to meet her too. I was sad but also excited as I would be revisiting a beautiful, much-remembered area which was and is comparable only to my magical childhood days by the banks of the mighty Brahmaputra.

It was winter and the drive through the plains of Assam is an experience no one should miss. I stopped at Kaziranga for lunch at the forest lodge atop a hillock before we drove on. Kaziranga is the home of the one-horned Rhino, a beautiful park established in 1905. An interesting story revolves around this park. Vicereine Mary Curzon visited the area in 1904, hoping to sight the one horned Rhino and was not able to do so. She immediately requested Lord Curzon to cordon off 152 square miles of the area to preserve this unique and endangered species. As we drove away, Kong Phris and I were remembering our elephant rides and the glorious sightings the park offered. By evening, we were in Dergaon. I had an early dinner with Papa when I was told that I must give Ram Bahadur a lot of hope and encouragement, not make anything obvious and make sure that Kong Phris does not burst into tears and give the game away. The doctors had been instructed to give him hope too and make him as comfortable and happy as possible.

After breakfast, sharp at 8 am, we started off and passed

Jorhat where I dropped off at Doss & Co to buy some chocolates and biscuits for Ram Bahadur—he liked Cream Crackers—and hoped to meet Sumita Doss, a school friend from Loreto Convent but she was not home. Then we carried on and as we drove through Dibrugarh, I thought of the Chatterjees, our vivacious Aunty Rani and her family, whose garden was in this 'tea city of India'. I remember driving into The Assam Medical College Hospital and coursing towards the Assam type building with a long verandah. It was an awful moment. To make it worse, the cops were waiting to see us in. Much as I was used to it, I could not really manoeuver my emotions well enough. Ram Bahadur came out, and with one look, I knew he knew. In his typical Gorkhali Hindi, he said, 'Hamara time aagaya Bibi Memsahib, koi baat nahin. Sab se badi baat hai ki aap log ke saath bees saal guzar gaya. Aur kya mangta hum ko?' *My time is up Bibi Memsahib, I am in the least bit concerned. But the good feeling is that I have been with all of you for twenty years. What more can I ask for?* He had tears in his eyes but upright and dignified. Kong Phris dug into her pla (her cloth bag for her kwai and tobacco) and strolled away swallowing her emotions. We sat for a while and I told him about Delhi and the heat, and my friends and all sorts of banter, my eyes shifting here and there and remarking on the hibiscus that flamed unabashedly in the corner. He unwrapped the biscuit packet I had brought and ate one and grinned, that special Ram Bahadur grin! We left soon after and as we drove off, I turned around. He waved, for the last time. So many people like Ram Bahadur crossed and enriched our lives and Papa remembered each one till his last days. In the tributes, you will read about them. They were the important people in my father's life because he found in them the sincerity and simplicity, unconditional love and straight forwardness which he treasured most in human relationships.

We passed Sibsagar and I so wanted to stop but I could not. Sivasagar was named after the big lake made by the Ahom king Siva Singha. The Ahoms ruled over Assam for 598 years from 1228-1826. This long and glorious reign was founded by the Mong Mao Thai prince, Sukaphaa. The Afghans and the Mughals were both repelled by the Ahoms and could never conquer Assam. The Ahom General, Lachit Borphukan thwarted the Mughals' last attempt to conquer Assam in the famous Battle of Saraighat in 1671. Sadly, there is no mention of this in any of our history books. The 'neglected Northeast' narrative continues to this day.

Then Jorhat came into view and I remembered our childhood in the century old SP's bungalow which was reputed to be haunted till my mother discovered that the nightly rattle that had been terrifying many occupants was the distant rumbling of the train rushing by. It was a happy posting in spite of the fact that we all had a bout of mumps. Our ever faithful and loving, Kong Lemsibon Nongrum took care of us and related stories that would divert our minds. She never forgot the evening ritual 'thang syrdep' (burning of coiled cotton cloth dipped in oil) to ward away negative energies and give us sound sleep.

The bungalow had a sprawling compound with open lawns all around. It was here that my two brothers, Bijon and Prabhat, age 5 and 4, were put on the saddle for the very first time. Earlier, when Mei expressed her apprehension that there may be an accident, Papa was said to have told her that he was 'going to make men of these boys'. He introduced the boys to the rough and tough ways of life—taught them the art of horse riding, trekking through miles and miles in the nearby tea gardens and encouraged them to play outdoor games. On the other hand, my sisters and I learnt from him the importance of dignity and excellence in every aspect of our lives, be it education, attire, etiquette, art, music and conversation. He was very particular about the way one spoke. He was delighted with the Loreto nuns when elocution was made compulsory. Parvati did miss her trots on Brenda the lovely chestnut mare, she confessed later, but those days one never questioned a parent's decision and Mei had decided 'no' to the daughters' horse riding.

My brothers on horseback in front of the SP's Bungalow in Jorhat (1956)

The Silchar Firing of 1960 was one incident which always filled my father with deep sorrow and remorse to the last days of his life. In his article on my father, Mr B.S. Baber had also written about it, 'In 1961, at Silchar during a popular agitation, Dey, then as DIG along with the Commissioner, Deputy Commissioner, the Superintendent of Police was commanding the District Police and CRPF contingent. Due to some misunderstanding, CRPF opened fire killing about 13 persons. Though Dey had not ordered the firing, he took all responsibility on his broad shoulders though he was not responsible.' (Article in Appendix H). It was during the Language agitation that riots had broken out in most parts of Assam. On that particular afternoon of May, it had turned violent and the situation was taking an ugly turn. A Junior Commission Officer of the Central Reserve Police Force started the firing in panic. Later when he realized his mistake, he begged for mercy but, expectedly, huge damage had been done. Although Papa had not ordered the firings, he took full responsibility being the senior most officer present in Silchar on that fateful day. It cost him a lot.

During the Judicial Inquiry, Siddhartha Shankar Ray, Barrister-at-law (later Chief Minister of West Bengal) represented the people. When Ray understood the inner story, the truth, he extricated him from the case and he and his wife, Maya Ray became good family friends.

Papa was exonerated from all the charges that were brought up before the Commission of Inquiry but the then Chief of the Intelligence Bureau noted in his personal file that he will not be awarded any police decorations or medal during his service. It was not this report that father was sad about. He was sad about the death of innocent young people. He told me, as he lay in his bed in Ganga Ram Hospital, during the last months of his life, 'There were young girls among the dead—young girls—and their parents were inconsolable. It was terrible. What followed this disaster—the inquiry and my not ever being considered for an award—seemed so small and insignificant compared to the tragedy that occurred. I will never forget it. I was not responsible for that firing but that is not the issue. I was there and could not prevent it. Those young girls… as you all were growing up the scene would come to me again and again. There were girls and women. To make matters worse I fell very sick. The doctors diagnosed it as thyroid. Do you remember my going to Calcutta with your grandmother to recuperate at Raja mama's house? Such an interesting man and the family took such good care of me.'

His maternal uncle used to sit with him in his garden for hours talking and when father grew restless, he would take out his favourite Rolls Royce and take him for a drive. Knowing his nephew's love of the outdoors, they would go to Victoria Memorial and the open greens around the Calcutta Race Course. There in the splendid grounds where nature and history merged with grace and majesty, my father began to heal.

It was only then, on an evening in Ganga Ram Hospital, New Delhi in 2001 that I learned why Siddhartha Shankar Ray had come with a battery of lawyers to our ancestral home at Umsohsun while my mother and her sisters and brothers sat in the library, not talking much. Parvati, Mayanti and I sat tremulously in our bedroom wondering what was happening as we were not told that the hearing for the Silchar firing was being held at home. Papa was too sick to move but insisted on being heard! I did not know until that day in May 2001, when I sat quietly at his bedside in Ganga Ram Hospital, as darkness came filtering into the room along with the tinkling of the temple bells and the azaan from the prayer complex below. I wanted to tell him that in the end it is all about destiny. How can I, however, convey this to a man who believed that you alone make or break your life and that you must accept it?

6

Of Commitment and Devotion

From Silchar, one crosses over to Mizoram where my father always had a wonderful time. He loved the Mizo sense of humour and straightforwardness. They and the other hill men would get away with so much from a man who could not tolerate stupidity and inertia and slip ups on duty. He would often narrate his drive with one of his drivers, Sarela. Papa had this idiosyncrasy about reaching his destined night halt come what may. He would not allow any deterrent to come in the way—weather, roads, an accident, a failed ambush, unexpected work or misadventures that may pepper a cop's life—nothing would. He would drive through the night and, being a foodie, would look forward to a pre-ordered dinner of rice, light dal, vegetables spiced with panchporon, fried fish and mutton curry. On one such drive, he had already been on the road for over ten hours and felt concerned for his Mizo driver, Sarela. So, he asked

Sarela if he was tired and if he should take over the wheel as he did not want him to fall asleep while driving. Sarela's reply was classic, 'Macchi ka aakhen kabhi bund hota hai?' *Does a fish ever close its eyes?* Sarela's reply notwithstanding, Papa got down and drove the rest of the way, chuckling now and again looking at an open-mouthed Sarela, in the back seat fast asleep. It was a story he would narrate every once in a while whenever he could bring it up in a conversation.

So many stories—how I wish I had written them down. How I wish I was more curious and interested! We, ignorant and innocent, however, took so many things for granted...

My brothers remember an incident soon after the Indo-Pak war of 1965. Papa was the Chief of the State Intelligence machinery when he got wind that young Mizo boys were crossing over to Pakistan for suspected training in weaponry. Nothing had been noticed at that point in time by the district authorities of the Lushai Hills. Father was not happy with the reports and decided that he would like to go and inspect and investigate himself. So, in December 1965, along with the Commandant of the 4th Battalion BSF, he decided he must go up to Aizawl, now the capital of Mizoram. My brothers Bijon and Prabhat accompanied him as it was during their school vacation. Little did they know that trouble was brewing in these majestic hills. They had lunch at Kolasib where Bijon overheard the officers report to Papa that young girls and boys were being taught a form of drill and it did not look as if they were practicing for the forthcoming Republic Day celebrations!

It was a fairly long meeting before the convoy set off for Aizawl. Prabhat was sitting in the last jeep which set off a little later and was carrying the provisions. On the way, they had a minor accident with a truck. The anti-outsider feeling was palpable by then. As soon as it happened, a group of Mizo boys jumped out and they were ready to attack the occupants with rods and sticks. An argument ensued between the driver Vaikhuma and the boys as Prabhat sat terror-stricken inside the jeep. Suddenly, he saw, to his utter relief, the boys retreating and backing off, getting into the truck and speeding away. It was only thanks to Vaikhuma that they were spared. Till now we do not know what he said to pacify them. Later in the evening, a dinner was hosted for my father by Major Hmingliana Tochhawng, a former colleague of fathers in the army and now an IAS officer, at his father, Pu Thanglula's house. During the course of the evening, it was discovered that the truck belonged to Major Tocchawng's brother-in-law, Lalhmingthanga, the son of the famous businessman and philanthropist, Pu Pachhunga.

Prabhat with Partei and his in-laws in Aizawl

Papa noted the incident but was least perturbed when it was reported to him earlier. He always believed that the Mizos were a people of honour and would not inflict injury on those fewer in numbers or who they thought were not of the same calibre. So, the party continued uninterrupted. That is another Mizo trait—they do not go on and on about negative occurrences. Life goes on, the party goes on. Before Papa left with the boys, Pu Thanglula held my father's hand and said, 'Pu Lala, I have many granddaughters. I hope one of your sons will, one day, marry one of them.' Little did he know that his future grandson-in-law would have been a causality that day if the driver Vaikhuma had not intervened when the young militants attacked the police jeep. Ten years down the line, his wish came true and my younger brother, Prabhat married Lalparliani—Partei to all of us—on 17th June 1976. Partei is the daughter of the beautiful Lalliani, sister of Major Hmingliana and the charismatic Pu Lalhmingthanga. Later, Bijon's son Atiar married Lalpeki Rialte, Partei's elder sister's daughter. They are now divorced but have a cordial relationship and the most charming and intelligent son, Rinzoa.

My father's affection for the local folk stemmed from his close interaction with them as a young boy. He admired them and imbibed from them the sterling qualities of genuineness and simplicity. He also enjoyed spending time with civil society. During his tours within and outside the state, he would take time off, to spend quality time with them and learn about local customs and way of life and their opinion on various subjects.

On his return to Shillong, Papa wrote a report and highlighted his findings and the indications of an impending rebellion. But it was too late! In the first week of February 1966, the first shot was fired and Aizawl, the District Headquarters of Lushai Hills, had been overrun by the fighters of the Mizo National Front. The Assam Rifles Battalion Headquarters was the only ground that government forces could hold on to. What followed thereafter is a history of shame to the Indian Union.

It all began with the Great Famine of 1950. The bamboo had flowered and the Mizos knew a famine was approaching. The Mizos refer to it as 'mautam'—bamboos dying. Once in every fifty years, the bamboos flower and also produce fruit after which the bamboos perish. The rats eat the fruits and multiply in multitudes. They in turn eat up all the crops and this results in a famine. The Mizos communicated this to the government which alerted New Delhi but it was left unheeded. On 1st March 1966, the Mizo National Front came under the leadership of Laldenga and a declaration of independence was made. The government took strong steps and by 25th March, the battle was all over the Lushai Hills. Violence continued until the peace talks in 1986 and the Peace Accord was signed. The story goes that Papa took canisters full of rosgullas to distribute, much to, I am sure, the Mizos' amusement!

Papa's humaneness was well known as much as his reputation as a dynamic and fearless cop. He was a man of strong likes and dislikes but if someone needed help, it was

Lala B.K. Dey presenting Commendation Certificate to a police officer of Kamrup District as Shri D.N.S. Shrivastava looks on.

Father with Shri I.P.M. and Shri B.K. Baruah

never denied. He would never let a friend down and no plea from anyone would ever go unheeded. During the Civil War in East Pakistan, mayhem reached fever pitch and violence, molestation and rape of women of all ages were rampant. The Pakistan Army was wreaking havoc under the command of General Tikka Khan. Thousands and thousands of refugees had crossed into Tripura, Assam and West Bengal. The Government of India was neck deep with problems of shelter and all the essential facilities. A vast sea of people fled into India terror-stricken and traumatized, most of them beyond repair. My father was then the Inspector General of Police of undivided Assam, steeped in work. One day, he received intimation from a former colleague of the Indian Civil Service that a friend and officer, who had served with Papa in the army and was settled in a tea garden in East Pakistan alongside the Indo-Pak border, had been murdered by the Mukti Bahini. His wife and children had been captured and kept captive in their camp on the Indian side, most probably in the town of Shella in Southern Khasi Hills. Once he confirmed the information, without a moment of hesitation, he sent word to the Commander of the Mukti Bahini that if they did not hand over the family immediately, he would be forced to drive them out of his territory. The family was rescued and brought up to Shillong and were handed over to the representatives of the Government of India after meeting my parents at our residence. The bereaved widow wanted to meet father to thank him. After a hearty breakfast, they wished her a happy future and safe journey via New Delhi ahead to Pakistan, where she wanted to resettle. My sister Parvati said she would never forget her face—a fair, oval-shaped face with light-coloured eyes filled with sadness. She spoke very little and left.

Soon after the war was over, Papa was summoned by my paternal great-grandmother, Tripura Sundari who was living in Shillong with Montu Mama, her younger son. She simply told him that she did not think that she had long to live and, therefore, he should immediately shift her back to Sylhet and that she must spend the last days of her life in her own home. My father did try to explain to her that it was not so easy as the post-war situation in the fledgling country of Bangladesh was not congenial, to which she replied that she thought her grandson was a 'big man' and for him, nothing could be impossible! My father knew he was left with no choice. It was the last wish of someone he adored and revered. After obtaining the required permission from the authorities of both countries, Papa picked her up on the morning of 12th January 1972, and drove directly to her bungalow in the tea garden in Sylhet. Jitendra Narayan Deb Choudhury, her eldest son, a renowned advocate and Papa's eldest maternal uncle was there to welcome her and take charge. Papa returned to Shillong early the following morning with mixed feelings of happiness and sadness. His grandmother was back home but he knew he would never see her again. My father's cousin, Kalyani Choudhuri, Kha Shipra, a highly respected and admired officer of the Indian Administrative Service in the West Bengal cadre, recollected the whole chain of events, 'Only Benuda could have done it, much to our relief and joy. He was something else, your father.' As she had wished, Tripura Sundari passed away peacefully in the family Estate home at Fenchuganj, Sylhet in the spring of 1973.

A commendable trait of my father's was his commitment to duty and what was right. It cost him a prestigious posting when he was the Superintendent of Police of the United Khasi and Jaintia Hills District with headquarters at Shillong. He was going home to Umsohsun when he was caught in a traffic jam on the Guwahati-Shillong Road, now known as U Tirot Sing Road. He waited for five minutes and then jumped out of his car to see what had caused the jam. There he saw the Chief Minister's wife busy window shopping from her car and shopkeepers were bowing backwards to serve her. He could not believe his eyes and that a person of that stature could break the law so brazenly. He was horrified and his sense of duty and responsibility did not allow him to waver, 'Please kindly move on, there is a traffic jam here!' he thundered to the driver. The occupants of the car were well aware who the voice belonged to. Within a few days, he received his marching orders and was transferred to Guwahati where my younger brother, Prabhat was born.

There is also another story which is a favourite because it always makes us laugh! My brother, Bijon was sitting in the Reserved Lounge in Delhi Airport waiting for a flight when a man walked in with his entourage. The receptionist at the Lounge introduced the gentleman to Bijon and they got chatting. He was an MP from Assam and was returning home from Delhi. In the course of the conversation, he asked Bijon if he was related to Lala B.K. Dey. My brother replied that he was his eldest son. The MP was delighted and related a story about his days in Cotton College. It was during the Language Agitation in Assam and the state was rife with violent protests. The students then were, naturally, drawn into this movement. One day, while he was in his room in the College Hostel, he suddenly heard students running down the corridor, shouting 'Bagh ahise dei! Bagh ahise!' *The tiger is coming! The tiger is coming!* There was utter panic and the students jumped out of windows, raced through the doors into corridors and ran out into the fields and into the bushes. Apparently, my father was known as 'the tiger'. Later, they learned that a very calm Lala Saheb had come on a routine visit with a posse of cops. They sighed with relief, the MP concluded, smiling. So did Papa when he heard the story. He chuckled, 'Naughty fellows!' Deep inside I think he always had a soft corner for the mischievous and rebellious young, a trait he shared with my mother and which I have inherited!

This tiger story reminded me of another tiger story about my father's great-great-grandfather, Jugal Kishore Ray Chaudhry. The story goes that, one evening, the villagers saw him drinking water from the river that ran through his father's estate. Not far from him was a tiger that was also quenching his thirst. Totally mesmerized, the people watched the scene with awe and terror. Once done, Jugal Kishore walked away calmly as the tiger continued to drink. I have a special feeling and respect for these magnificent creatures and I love this story.

The officers and his bosses relied a lot on my father and his somewhat fearsome personality in order to control a volatile situation. During the Hill State Movement of the 1960s, Papa was DIG in charge of the International Border with East Pakistan and was away in the Garo Hills Sector when trouble escalated in the capital city. It was the winter of 1963. The police had to resort to firing and a man was killed on the spot at Motphran, the centre of the main market. The government was in a state of panic as never before had such a crisis happened in Shillong—police firing into a mob and killing a civilian. The Inspector General of Police, Mr Imdad Ali, sent an urgent message to my father via the wireless

Imdad Ali IP taking the salute at a BSF Investiture Parade. Also seen in the picture is my father and Lt. Col. Chotu Singh Rathore. (1963)

to return to headquarters immediately. Father rushed back through the night to find the town silent as a tomb. Curfew had been imposed. The IGP was relieved with his arrival and after the customary salute, he shook Papa's hand and said, 'Good you are back.' Papa, however, was extremely distressed with the turn of events and wished he had been in Shillong before the unprecedented incident. Little did he know that such firings would become an everyday occurrence until the present times.

In the later part of the 1960s and early 1970s, our frontier—A Land Of Beauty And Grace—was engulfed by insurgencies and public protests, which very often led to clashes between members of the public and government agencies and a growing demand of the hill people for self-governance within the framework of the Indian Constitution. The insurgent movements in Nagaland and the Lushai Hills, where the hill tribes had put up their banner for complete independence from the Indian Union, was being dealt with by the Central Government. The Assam Police, however, had its hands full with other problems.

In 1972, my father had actually toyed with the idea of premature retirement having completed a tenure of almost three years as the Police Chief. He had, at that time, reached the pinnacle of his career and he felt it would be unfair to the service and to his juniors if he continued at the helm for the remaining eight years of his service. Somehow, however, he did not. 1972 was the year when two administrative districts were carved out of composite Assam, to make Meghalaya the twenty-first state in the Indian Union. The seat of power of the government had to shift out of Shillong after more than hundred years. It was a sad moment for many, and more so for my father. He had to 'lead the charge'—moving the police headquarters to its temporary location in Guwahati, reallocating his officers and personnel and, most importantly, in assisting the Government of Assam to tide over the shock and the pressure of shifting an entire capital city. There is always a time for everything and we cannot avoid destiny.

My mother, in her inimitable way, took it all in her stride. She always said that to be a good policeman's wife, one had to be calm, easy and have a sense of humour. She would not blink an eyelid if father had to suddenly rush off and leave a carefully prepared tea or meal, a toast half-eaten, a perfect roast left untouched. She would rather enjoy the stories that he would bring back home. There is one story which she would often relate about Mr K.P.S. Gill, which used to make her laugh again and again.

Apparently, when Mr Gill was the Superintendent of Police of the United Khasi and Jaintia Hills District, with its headquarters in the state capital Shillong, a thief was caught and brought to his office for questioning. This particular offender was in and out of jail and had a gift of the gab until he met his match, in a different way! During questioning, he kept avoiding the answers and was, in his usual style, going round in circles. Finally, Uncle Gill, fed up and infuriated, stood up from his chair and shouted, 'U thok!'—meaning that he is lying. The thief who was five feet nothing and had,

1.

2.

3.

4.

1. The penultimate gathering of senior police officers with Chief Minister Sarat Chandra Sinha in front of the Secretariat in Shillong. (1972) **2.** On parade at Garrison Ground Shillong. **3.** Bidding farewell to police personnel who were transferred to the state of Meghalaya. (31st May 1972) **4.** The last get-together at Shillong of senior police officers of Assam before shifting of the capital. (May 1972) till then, been facing the officer only waist upwards was so shocked to see this huge, towering figure that he keeled over backwards and fainted.

Aunty Herminder Gill was my mother's close friend and great support in my father's latter years in Guwahati. My parents who were unable to live in Guwahati without the Brahmaputra had moved to a newly built cottage next to the SP's quaint and exquisite abode preferring it to the official residence my father was allocated. Mei was ailing by then, but they had a merry little Ladies' Club consisting of Aunty Rahman, Aunty Borbora, Aunty Gill and the wives of a few young officers. So many of my Assamese friends and their parents also visited my mother in those difficult days and Mei always remembered them with great affection.

I remember them too, and the mighty Brahmaputra which left a deep impression on me when I was barely three, growing up in the SP's bungalow. Brahmaputra, the Son of Brahma, the ninth longest river in the world taking its 3848 km of ever- changing hues and moods as it travels from Tibet through India and Bangladesh on its long journey to the Bay of Bengal. To me, it remains to this day as one of the most divine and magical manifestations of God, the Creator.

End of Innings. Saying goodbye to the officers of Assam Police upon his retirement as Shri K.P.S. Gill looks on. (31st December 1978)

7

Preparing for the Third Innings

In the afternoon of 31st December 1978, my father retired from government service having served—the colonial government during the period of the Raj as a 'royal gunner' and the Government of India as an officer of the Indian Police Service—for thirty-six years. At the end of these wonderful years of challenges and acclaim, he bade farewell to the uniform with a sense of fulfillment, having had the good fortune of associating with two different aspects of world and Indian history. After attending the official ceremonies and the farewell parade by the Assam Police at the Guwahati Police Reserve Lines, he got into his car and sped up the Guwahati-Shillong Road to face the third innings in his life—retirement.

So, he arrived in Shillong on that winter's day, happy but with many thoughts in his mind. My mother gave him full support by simply saying, 'Time will tell.' This was Mei's favourite phrase and it always gave us all the much-needed breathing space in times of crisis. We, the children, were all living in Umsohsun then at my maternal grandmother's sprawling estate.

Meirad, Hinimon Jaid Dkhar Sawian, daughter of the iconic educationist and social reformer, Babu Jeebon Roy of the Mairom clan, was married to Ely Manik Syiem of the Mylliem royal family. They had five children: Pisimon, Lisimon, Maham Singh, Sitimon and Kynpham Singh. Parad Ely Manik passed away after just ten years of marriage. Meirad was so devastated she never stepped out of the house again. Yet she never showed her sadness or let it affect those around her. She taught me acceptance, humility and kindness by sheer example.

Family photograph at Umsohsun with my maternal grandmother, Meirad (1958)

Her original family home had collapsed under the fury of the Great Earthquake of 12th June 1897 and her father, Babu Jeebon Roy constructed another residence to accommodate his huge extended family who were staying in the chicken coops. He procured the best furniture shipped from England to fill his new home. Meirad created a world of her liking once she stepped in as the khadduh, the youngest daughter and custodian of the family property. She developed the Northern part, where Parad Jeebon Roy had established a printing press, into an orchard of citrus fruits; the South had three cottages amidst plum and pear trees; the West had a wall dividing our compound with our neighbours' who were also relatives from the Mairom clan; the East accommodated the cow sheds. Unlike most of the local people, she enjoyed milk and milk products and encouraged the entire family and staff to include it in their diet. She planted many exotic trees that interspersed the flowering jacarandas and gulmohurs and flower beds with a plethora of flowers—each season the garden wore a different hue. Meirad only ate the rice that came from her paddy fields in Sumer, the fruits and vegetables from her garden and the milk from her own cows. My parents, even after they moved to Mawprem, enjoyed the fragrant Joha and Manipuri rice from Sumer till the last days of their lives.

Meirad lived in self-imposed 'purdah'. Her outings were limited to drives and visits to close relatives on special occasions. If she wanted shoes, they would be brought to her doorstep and the same went for clothes and other requirements.

In spite of this protected existence, Meirad was broadminded because Umsohsun was the hub of intellectual thought and ideas where people gathered and discussed world politics, philosophy and of course, nationalism and Independence. This freed her from the narrow physical confines of her privileged life to dimensions that made her a thinking and educated woman way beyond her times. Mei told me that one of her wishes was that she would, one day, have the whole of India under her roof, a sentiment which she shared with my father. She did. Seven of her grandchildren, including us five siblings, have married outside our community, what in common parlance is referred to as 'love marriage'.

My parents on their wedding day; my mother in our traditional wedding attire. (14th March 1949)

Mei and Papa's too was a love story that began almost a century ago when a seven-year-old boy from Sylhet, while travelling up to these hills, vowed that he must meet Sib Charan Roy, the man who, according to the khoh porters, the nongkitbriew, owned all the lands that they passed through from Sylhet and up the slopes. He recalled that his first impression of my mother was of a fierce hockey player when they used to gather to play in the Umsohsun compound. Funnily, Mei also talked of her initial connect with Papa and remembered the 'legs that were thinner than mine.' She was very proud of her rather ample legs which were very much like her regal paternal aunts and she did not mind being teased for her 'khohwah Mylliem'.

She adored her aunts and often visited them in the settlements of Madanriting and Laitkor at the outskirts of Shillong. My paternal and maternal families got along famously right from the beginning due to their common interests in intellectual discourse and the Sylhet connection. My mother's family's zamindaris, Kalasadok and Batrai were situated in Sylhet District. Somewhere along the way, my grandmother had decided on Papa as a prospective son-in-law. They were married on 14th March 1949. Theirs was the first civil marriage of these hills.

Although my father belonged to a fiercely male dominated patriarchal family, he gave us—his children—the space to grow and develop on the lines of my mother's society, which is matrilineal. Matriliny is different from matriarchy. In Matriliny, lineage is taken from the mother but the head of the family is the eldest maternal uncle. Papa told me before I left for Delhi University that it was a decision he took along with my maternal uncles. He did not want us to grow up confused and have a crisis of identity. Nevertheless, he maintained a close and strict supervision over us as children. Our growing up years were packed with travel, adventure

Grandfather Lala Bijoy with Grand Uncle Chandranath Roy and Rashmohan Roy of Hima Sohra

and interesting episodes. I have seen the length and breadth of Assam, visited some of the unique places in the country and met many interesting people from different parts of the world. My parents groomed us into what they termed as 'international citizens'—no caste, no creed, no prejudices of any sort including class. We were taught that all living beings were the children and creation of the Almighty and must be respected as such.

It so happened that at that point in time when Papa was preparing for retirement, his friend and brother-in-law, my maternal uncle, Maham Singh had decided that my grandmother's dairy farm had to move out of Umsohsun and knowing my father's passion for animals, especially cows, horses and dogs, he gave Papa the offer he could not refuse. The cows were moved to Mawprem which was one of the properties the family owned. It was later named after my

Shri B.K. Nehru with my mother and her sister Sitimon Sawian in Umsohsun

youngest sister, Nayantara Lakyrsiew (Lakyrsiew—Awakened—is her second name) because our family won a major court case soon after her birth. This beautiful estate sits on two hillocks and stretches westwards onto the grassy acres that gradually dip into the gorges below where, in the monsoon, waterfalls abound.

It was a magical refuge for my father. There, among his grazing cattle and ponies, with the hills in the distance and nothing else but the sky and earth, he found his peace. 'I would never give up this life for anything in the world,' he would say as offers of various post retirement assignments poured in. And it was here in Lakyrsiew that my parents would build which was then one of the most beautiful homes in the Northeast. It was like a gift from my grandmother for a much-loved son-in-law. She was the one who had decided that he marry my mother. We never got to know if she was aware that my father was in any case very much in love with Mei. When the formal proposal of marriage was received when he returned home after the Great War, Meirad was all set to fly them to

England to solemnize a civil marriage if the procedure was not possible in India due to the prevailing laws.

Arjun Trivedi, the son of one of my parents' favourite couples, Dr S.A. Trivedi and Dr Geeta Mehta (Uncle Satyen and Geeta Pishimash to me), vividly recollected Papa planning the house. 'He was very particular that each room should have a view of the spectacular landscape of his land. He was also very sure about the necessity of fireplaces in the rooms and pondered fondly on how everyone would be enjoying the blazing fires in the winters ahead.

He wanted fruit trees of all the fruits that grow in Shillong and vegetables too. The cow sheds were to be given pride of place on a separate hill. I always enjoyed his company and the way he would call me Arjie. My siblings Shankar, Bhairav, Gauri and I miss him a lot. Aunty Lisimon concentrated on the garden, what would grow where in different seasons. She was meticulous in her planning; calmly and with a smile she walked around instructing.'

The detailed layout of the house was done by my brother, Prabhat who was then a student of the Delhi School of Planning and Architecture. The garden was laid out by my parents with the able assistance of my middle sister, Parvati who also did the interiors of the rooms. They made Step Gardens in the style reminiscent of the Emperor Babur's 'Char Bagh' and archways where rambling roses climbed and cascaded in gorgeous blooms during the early summer well into autumn. The driveway was flanked by mauve and pink hydrangeas and bushes of azaleas. It was then reputedly one of the most beautiful gardens this side of the Brahmaputra! When Governor M.M. Jacob heard of a garden that was lovelier than the Raj Bhavan, he was intrigued. On his first visit to Lakyrsiew, along with his niece and her children, he did say he could not refute the remark and must admit that the tea was even better as was the scintillating conversation with the family members.

Mawprem was famous for its breakfast and high teas. By then, my parents would avoid dinners as their routine had changed completely to light food, quiet evenings and early nights. Mei with her maids and serials, Papa with his news from the BBC and Doordarshan and, afterwards, movies on the DVD player with a roomful of his favoured live-in staff. I remember his friend and fellow IPS officer, Bah Zaman, CZ Ghafoor bringing him a carton of classic movies whenever he visited Lakyrsiew. Father was partial to guests who liked milk and could consume a decent amount without fuss. Breakfast began with a bowl of papaya and followed by porridge, with cut bananas, raisins and almonds (for those who enjoy these) and milk—lots of it! My two brothers-in-law, highly intelligent and vibrant men, lovers of lavish breakfasts and extended debates enjoyed this morning spread enormously. Mohan Srinivasan won hands down with his penchant for papaya, pineapple and Cherrapunji bananas and milk which was not diluted like one had to for some guests, much to my father's displeasure! Geert Linnebank, the youngest son-in-law with his great appetite for Richmond ham won the non-veg award especially when he proclaimed that the ham was as good as any of the best in Europe. Toast and tea would round up the meal. Toast of Mahari bread and only Mahari bread was served and Assam tea with a few leaves of Darjeeling put right at the end just before pouring. After years in the North, I have completely turned to dhaba chai and when my parents were alive it would be made for me almost surreptitiously. It was not difficult because I always have tea by myself, everywhere, after a long siesta.

The imposing and genteel Shri L.P. Singh was another Governor who was close to my father and he and his family would drop by for tea and enjoy the spectacular sunsets. When I married in 1974, he most graciously extended a helping hand in the many intricate formalities of a Rajput wedding. My husband, Alark Singh belongs to the Sirmaur royal family of Himachal. It turned out to be a splendid wedding with all the inputs we received from Mr L.P. Singh and the Charkhari family with whom my father shared his enduring love for animals especially with the youngest son, M.K. Jaibir and his cousin, Princess Kriti of Tripura. The humorous incident of one of my husband's friends from Junga in Himachal Pradesh would be related again and again after the wedding. Apparently, after downing one too many, most normal and expected at a Rajput wedding, a very jolly and garrulous Kanwar Pradip Sen of Junga walked up to the Governor and started chatting with him. In the midst of the conversation he asked His Excellency, Mr L.P. Singh, 'And what do you do for a living?' Without blinking an eyelid, the Governor replied very gently, 'I work here.' At this point, a cousin who was close by joined them and nudged Pradip and revealed the person's identity. Pradip remembered his inebriation evaporating very quickly as he looked up at an imposing man, smiling at him, enigmatically. Such was the class and calibre of the man! Pradip Sen quietly slunk away and continued the party in safer grounds with my thoroughly amused cousins. Apparently, the Governor also shared the joke and had a good laugh later on.

8

What a Wonderful Life

'What a wonderful life!' is one phrase that my father often repeated, and my mother would smile in agreement. It was usually after a few hours on the other hill where the horses and cows were grazing and the wind whistled through the pines, the distant hills framed against the azure sky. Father had a special spot where he would sit and enjoy this bounty. 'Kmie I Bibi,' he would say when he returned, 'what a wonderful life!' They would always refer to each other not by name but in the traditional Khasi terms—Kmie I Bibi and Kpa I Bibi. Bibi is me, their first born. His brothers-in-law were 'kynum' and Meirad was 'kiaw'. This chapter hopes to capture that period in their lives and also the days of steed and soirees and nights around the crackling fire which seemed to never end.

My father's deep connect with and love for horses was well known. He was so happy when Bijon married Aneeta,

Memorial stone of Mohan Lal in Guptipara, Hooghly, where he spent his last days.
Mohan Lal was the last Dewan of Bengal, Bihar and Orissa.

The author's maternal grandmother's residence in Umsohsun where she grew up.

Glimpes of the home in Lakyrsiew belonging to the author's parents.

Family home at Fenchuganj, Sylhet.

Lala Bimal Kumar Dey's ponies at the Lakyrsiew estate.

The author and her son with indigenous wild ponies in the grassland of West Khasi Hills, 1983.

War medals awarded to Major Bimal Kumar Dey, 1939, 45 Star Burma Star.

The Lala Dey Trophy was instituted in 2002 and has been an integral part of the IPS Equestrian Meet all over India.

Lala B.K. Dey's Grandchildren. Clockwise from top: Atiar, Larsing, Salim Kordor, Lyndan, Hammarsing, Saasha Bakor, Hanut and Boris, Saurabh, Lukhimai and Larimon.

Lala B.K. Dey's great-grandchildren

the daughter of Vice Admiral Robin Batra and Mrs Mira Batra. It was not only because of her intelligence and beauty but because she was a keen rider. I accompanied them once on their rides in the Golf Links and up to Umpling. I was in the car and it was a captivating sight to see Aneeta on Isabella, Nayan on Kanhaiya and Papa on Jaffer riding across the rolling greens up to the wind-swept forests of pines up to Umpling. At the end of the ride, Papa helped Aneeta to dismount from her horse and with a smile on his face told

(Above): On horseback—My father in the centre, Aneeta to his right and Nayantara to his left. (Right): Welcoming President Fakhruddin Ali Ahmed at the wedding reception of my brother, as the beautiful bride, Aneeta looks on.

her, 'Now you can marry my son!' Later, he jokingly teased my mother, 'I married you not only for your beauty but because your grandfather owned a fine stable.' Parad Jeebon Roy used to ride to work on his white steed when he was the Senior Extra Assistant Commissioner in the late nineteenth century, just before the Great Earthquake of 1897, with Mr J.C. Arbuthnot as the Deputy Commissioner. My father too would often ride to office in Shillong. Once, when he rode into the premises of the State Assembly, this 'misdemeanour' came up for Question by a Member of the Opposition. When the matter was referred to police headquarters for their comments, a reply was furnished thus, 'A police officer is authorized to travel by any mode of transport to attend to his duties.' The matter was put to rest. Later, of course, he realized it was attracting too much attention and affecting the traffic and reluctantly reverted back to his official car. He would insist though that official cars were in any case a nuisance with the cavalcade of cars and red lights and incessant cacophony. I think he basically liked to be in-charge and being driven around was not his cup of tea! On longer drives out of the city, he would often take to the wheel. Glowing images of him flash by as I write: his change of expression and his smile as he raced through those rain-washed roads in undivided Assam, totally in command. I would then imagine him galloping on his horse with the same aura. I still do.

It was also because of horses and riding that the Governor Mr B.K. Nehru and my father got along so well. The Raj

Bhavan in Shillong, the residence of the Governor of Assam was very different from its counterparts of the other states of India. The Governor of Assam was vested with special powers and he had the authority to overrule decisions taken by the State Government on certain matters. He was also the Head of the Government that administered the Northeast Frontier Agency (NEFA), now the state of Arunachal Pradesh. He could under the Constitution assume the powers and functions of the different Tribal District Councils. Unlike his contemporaries in other states, he was definitely not a 'figure head'. As corollary, the members of the political executive were more than just respectful to the Institution of the Raj Bhavan.

It was but natural, therefore, that the Government of India would appoint persons of eminence as the Governor of this remote and far-flung territory of the Indian Union which had its own form of autonomy till the 1970s.

Mr B.K. Nehru, debonair and affable with his patrician good looks, was a former denizen of the Diplomatic Core. He had the inborn tact and experience to draw upon the knowledge and inputs of both a mixture of individuals, personalities and agencies of the government without necessarily, having to rely entirely on the structure of established bureaucracy.

My father Lala B.K. Dey as a senior police officer was not only an authority on security matters pertaining to the composite state of Assam but had a deep insight, knowledge and understanding of issues social, administrative and strategic that pertained to the neighboring states of Manipur and NEFA—particularly the tribal inhabited areas. His insight was way beyond the general bookish knowledge of the land and its people. Mr B.K. Nehru, very often, drew upon my father's understanding of the pertinent issues that governed the facts, behavioral patterns, sensitivities and the varying socio-political constructs that the tribal communities had lived with for centuries in this area of the sub-continent.

Explaining his dairy project to Governor B.K. Nehru

Mr B.K. Nehru also discovered something special which they shared in common with his IGP and that was his love for horses and riding. Mr Nehru and Papa would often set off on horseback deep into the pine forests that skirted the capital city. They would ride along the century old bridle paths for hours together. This companionship grew into a bond both official and social. In these marvelous hours on horseback, they would discuss many issues pertaining to Northeast India. Many were resolved under the open skies as they trotted along undisturbed, unperturbed. Besides he also took keen interest in my father's pet project of raising a dairy suitable to the hilly terrain of the Khasi Hills where a strain of Jersey and Holstein cattle were bred to adapt to the peculiar climatic conditions that prevailed in these hills. He would very often visit Lakyrsiew with his family and spend quality time at the farm over hot cups of tea.

Beyond these tracks into the breathtakingly beautiful countryside of West Khasi Hills, Papa would ride with Bah Ming Kurbah and Bah Wilo Kharmawlong. They were the quintessential Khasi rural folk whose company my father enjoyed enormously. He was keen to identify a particular breed of indigenous horses which he wanted to preserve. I remember accompanying him to Rangshken along with my young son, Salim Kordor Singh. It was an unforgettable trip into the Khasi countryside. It began with us relishing a typical Khasi lunch in Bah Ming's home, where rice and a watery dal was served with fried fish and phansdieh, potato fries for Papa and boiled pork with herbs and dried fish chutney for me. Thus well fortified we set off and drove to the horse market. What a picturesque spot it was, with rolling hills, the colour of wet moss and a gurgling stream running through, sparkling silver—it was so clear! Many idyllic hours were spent there with my father patting and talking to the horses and their owners like old friends. On the way back, we visited my Marbaniang cousins in Tyrsat village, children of my handsome and colourful Pakhynnah Tulu, Lala Tulsi Kumar Dey and Nah Medolis.

Aunty Fori, Mrs Shobha Nehru, charming and vibrant also became part of our lives. She would drop by for tea and ask about Khasi culture and tradition and several other questions, some which were not easy to answer. One was—why do the Khasis have no Art as in paintings and so on? It intrigued her as she was fond of Art, was a great collector and gave illuminating lectures on World Art to my sister, Parvati. My younger uncle Kynpham Singh was the only one who could give a satisfactory answer which she accepted, somewhat—that we are surrounded with so much natural beauty that we did not feel the need to replicate it, rather just admire and revere it. She would have certainly appreciated the great outburst of artistic talent now prevalent in Shillong.

The drawing room in Umsohsun is exactly as it was in those long-ago days. Those days when Papa and Mama had musical evenings with the Duaras and Nazirs, Bah Stanley Nichols Roy and his charming wife, Aunty Helen, where the music of Beethoven and Bach, Chopin and Mozart floated out of the lace curtains billowing in the wind. Over tea accompanied by cucumber and egg sandwiches and Mahari cakes and, of course, jalebis and shondesh from Delhi Mistan—Papa would never miss his mithais—they would discuss the nuances of different compositions in great detail. And small trivia too like—was Antonio Salieri responsible for Mozart's death and so on. Sometimes, my aunt, Sitimon would perform and play the piano. As a young girl, I thought nobody played Beethoven's Fur Elise the way she did. Sometimes, a record would be played on the gramophone and Maro Lanza's Ave Maria would fill the air with pure magic.

Parvati says that she perfected the art of conversation then when she and cousin Mayanti were made to sit at the back on the Queen Anne chairs during the soirees. From childhood, of course, traditional Khasi etiquette had been taught to us on how to eat, drink, sit, walk, talk and so on. My father was also extremely particular about how one spoke and pronounced the words be it English or Khasi. We knew no Hindi then. Mayanti, laughingly, recalls that most of those evenings were a blur to her because she knew that soon she would be asked to play either Besame Mucho or La Paloma as a closure to the evening, every single evening! The boys were seldom asked to join, not after Prabhat and Marphrang giggled unabashedly when a famous French soprano, a special invitee sang Madame Butterfly. That was an unforgettable evening but the boys' behaviour still makes us blush! The sofa, the lamp behind it and the bookcase where the French singer stood are still exactly as they were over half a century ago.

Pasan Ken (Kendro Mohan Diengdoh) and my mother's cousin, San Twilsibon Phanbuh who lived close by would often drop in after supper. Pasan Ken was the dynamic coal baron of the Northeast and a successful businessman. San Twil would sit with the ladies in the small sitting cum dining room adjoining the kitchen, Pasan and my father and Mamas would discuss politics in the drawing room. Very often they would be joined by my mother's cousin's husband, Bah Nor Singh Nongbri, a smart and well-read bureaucrat and, of course, our effervescent Pasan Hipshon Roy if he was not in NEFA (now Arunachal Pradesh) where he was posted as an officer of the Indian Frontier Administrative Service.

During the Hill State Movement in the late 1960s, discussions would continue well into the night. This Movement was started by Mr Hoover Hynniewta, Captain Williamson Sangma, my father's classmate in school Mr Stanley Nichols Roy and others of the All Party Hill Leaders Conference. The Khasis, Jaintias and Garos had demanded for creation of a separate state for the tribals.

They, like all the different ethnic tribes in the Northeast, felt that progress and upliftment projects can only be implemented if they were granted the right to administer and govern themselves. I remember Mama Maham being concerned about the new land transfer acts and trade licenses. He felt that we needed people from outside for optimum development and feared unemployment and the calamitous consequences of this malaise involving our youth. He always felt concerned for the young, especially those who are economically challenged and those in rural areas.

In 1972, the state of Meghalaya was carved out of Assam. Mornings were special to my father. He would be woken up by the bagpiper during the Change of Guards in the house. Morning tea was sipped listening to the All India Radio, the news read by Pamela Singh and Latika Ratnam. He was partial to both as they spoke perfect English. This was followed either by Mira bhajans or the Carnatic renderings of Dr N Ramani, while he got ready. When he sat down for breakfast, the bagpiper would station himself behind the guava tree opposite the verandah and play the highland lilts and would continue to do so till father left home for work.

Umsohsun was also famous for its food. My father was a connoisseur of fine dining. After Tafajur, the Muslim cook left everyone was tested and tried. The formidable Kmie I Win won best mutton, Balwant Singh, the valet, the mutton chops prize and Kong Lem the best chicken curry cooked the Cherrapunji style which is somewhat like what is known in recipe books as Chicken Dak Bungalow. Vegetables would be spiced with either panchporon or simple steamed with some butter. Fish dishes, of course, were aplenty with hilsa sorso mach, katla morighonto, and fried fresh rohu or bhekti ever present but only on intimate sit-down dinners.

Otherwise crumbly fish cutlets were the preferred dish to suit a buffet. Salads were seldom given importance and would squat in the corner of the enormous table as mere decorative pieces but an array of homemade pickles and tok, a tomato chutney with dates were always served. My father was partial to payesh and rasmalai (called Horibhog in Shillong those days) from Delhi Mistan Bhandar, as desserts but fruits in season with cream—especially peeled Cherrapunjee oranges—and caramel custard were always served as well.

For his Sunday lunches, his first preference would be to his parents' home or to his brother's, Wing Commander L.C.K. Dey. Pakhynnah Chitu's wife, Aunty Parul's fish preparations and mutton korma were incomparable. Those were idyllic afternoons because Pakhynnah Chitu and his four children, Ranjana, Ravi, Ajay and Sonali lived in the most charming house behind the Raj Bhavan, nestled amidst pines. Ranjana is a worthy successor of her mother and I remember how Papa used to relish the food she used to bring to the hospital in Delhi.

My father's other great passion was not just good food but organizing feasts at home where he would watch with delight people relishing and wolfing their meal. Small eater and diet conscious guests were not his favourites! He was not a religious and ritualistic man. As I mentioned earlier, his worship was by performing his duties and being kind to all and also the flora and fauna which he connected so deeply with. During the Durga Puja celebrations, however, his yearly visit to Ramakrishna Mission to pay his obeisance to the Goddess Durga and partake in the festivities on asthami was a must. Back home a feast would be prepared for the entire family and anyone who dropped by. His guests of honour were his staff. His favourite cousin, Pakhynnah Pradip (Dey Chaudhuri) was a regular participant much to my mother's joy for she liked him immensely. Papa would also go to the Hindu Mission in Mawprem where he was the President for many years.

On Eid, father would not miss Aunty Saleha Rahman's incomparable biryani. Christmas would be spent doing the rounds to the homes of all his childhood friends. Bah Kenny, the local grocer was a favourite stop for a cup that cheers laced with memories of his carefree boyhood days.

A family visit to the Taj Mahal. Me, Prabhat, Bijon, Nayantara and Parvati with parents.

LAKYRSIEW. Memorable moments frozen in time

Clockwise from top left

PK Dey Chowdhuri -a favourite cousin

Governor LP Singh with his

ADC Captain Biren Borgohain

General OP Malhotra with Father

Brigadier AP Dutta (VC) and his wife, Nanda

Chief Secretary NK Rustomji & Vice Admiral

RN Batra

INDIAN BOUQUET.

A Short Prayer.

Almighty Lord of time and space,
  Of brute and thing inert,
Of man endowed with every grace,
  Of head and soul and heart!

From mountain down to bubbling froth,
  Do all thy hand declare;
From Brahma down to short-lived moth,
  Do all thy kindness share.

In Bible, Veda and Koran,
  Religious books of old,
Jehova, Alla and Brahman,
  Though thou hast long been called;

Yet Thou unknowable and unknown,
  Without a form or name;
Never to die, wast never born,
  Shalt ever be the same.

Thy throne is not in Moslem Vehst,
  In Heaven or Baikunt;
But now and ever thou dost rest
  In Bhakta's heart untaint.

Thou lovest all that hourly pray,
  And all that execrate,
And all that do thy' hest obey,
  And all that do thee hate.

2

As Buddha dost thou save the east,
  As Jesus Christ, the west,
As Mahammad, all the land betwixt,
  King Bharat's tract except.

The Hindus know Thy diverse name:
  Nrishingha, Krishna, Ram;
Adore thee they with vedic hymn
  Or loud-sung Harinam.

Eternal source of Forces Three
  Called Brahma, Vishnu, Siv,
Thyself thou keepest perfect free
  From all that in thee doth live.

Alas! the day when once my soul
  Did live as part of thine;
O it was then how pure and whole,
  Unlike this tainted *mine*!

When, when again, Lord, Maya's veil
  Wilt kindly take away?
When, when again my *jiv* will hail
  That long lost blessed day?

I wish not either Kuver's pelf
  Or Ravan's palace fine;
But grant that this my little self
  May soon be part of Thine.

Written by my great-grandfather Lala Prasanna Kumar Dey

9

Riding into the Sunset

Father's health deteriorated once he returned from New Delhi in May 2001. When he knew he may have to be on life support, he stopped eating. No amount of coaxing worked. On 9th July 2001, an ISKON group from Nadia suddenly arrived to sing bhajans. To this day, we do not know who called them and how they suddenly arrived in Lakyrsiew. They sang throughout the night and left at the crack of dawn. My mother said she noticed my father's face soften into a smile throughout and thought he may even miraculously recover as she left his room that night. A few hours after the singers left, however, Papa breathed his last. It was a lovely July morning; the lagerstroemia was blazing a glorious purple and the rain-soaked earth had that special aroma of freshness. My siblings and cousins rushed in soon after; slowly, everyone arrived and surrounded his bed. Nayantara held his hand and I his feet; he had beautiful feet. I knew it was my mother's toilet time so I took a little while before I went to her room. 'Mei, Papa is at peace,' I whispered, hugging her. She knew and she was grateful that her childhood friend, her husband, the love of her life will not have to suffer anymore. They both dreaded a life of being bed-ridden and dependent. Her eyes filled up and she said choking but clear and strong, 'I know. Call Nepal immediately. All the rituals must be done perfectly. Nothing should be left out.' Nepalda is a relative of Papa's from Sylhet who was very clued up about rituals unlike my father.

The funeral was held a day later. His two horses with their stirrups crossed over took precedence over the family priests and led the funeral procession. A contingent of the Assam Police, which was deputed from Guwahati, gave him the General Salute. The guns were fired and ripped the air as the huge crowd that had gathered stood in respectful silence. The Buglers sounded the Last Post that pierced through the sombre stillness as his two sons and his eldest grandson lit the pyre.

He was cremated on the second hilltop of Lakyrsiew where he would often sit and watch the quiet hills in the distance and the spectacular sunsets of the monsoon months. On that July evening, he rode into the limitless horizon for the last time. That was how it felt as the flames leaped up to the open sky.

And life, for us, was never the same again.

Lakyrsiew

Epilogue

Mr H.S. Chittaranjan, former Director General of Police of Assam and Meghalaya, had written the following to the eldest son, Bijon:

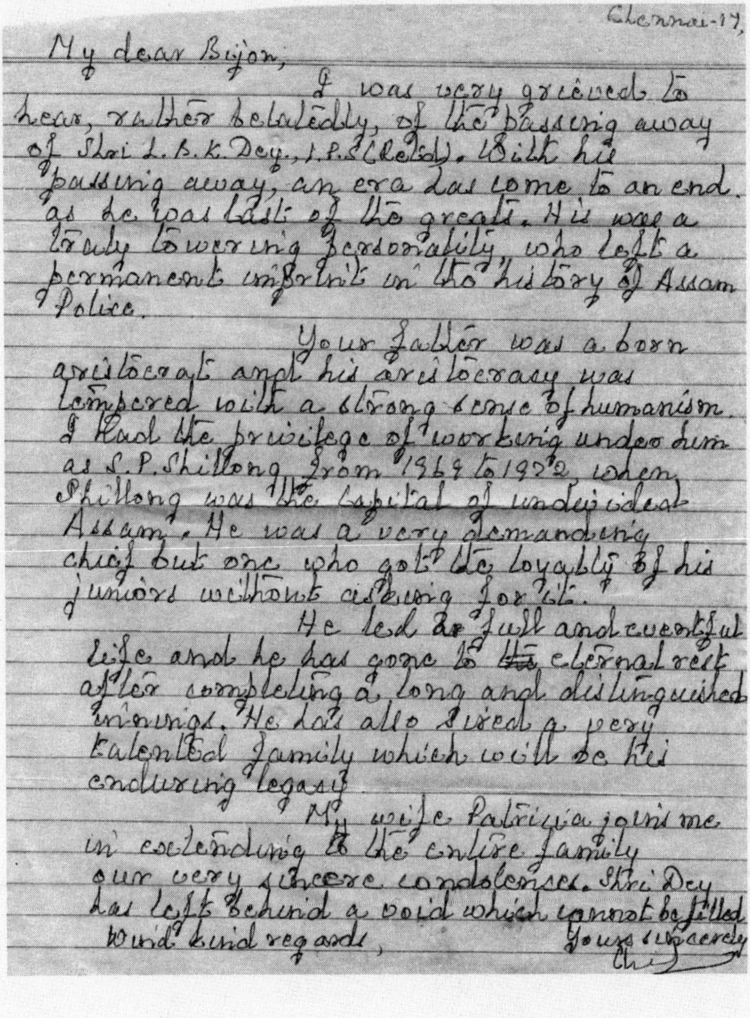

Chennai-17,

My dear Bijon,

I was very grieved to hear, rather belatedly, of the passing away of Shri L.B.K. Dey, I.P.S (Retd). With his passing away, an era has come to an end as he was last of the greats. His was a truly towering personality, who left a permanent imprint in the history of Assam Police.

Your father was a born aristocrat and his aristocracy was tempered with a strong sense of humanism. I had the privilege of working under him as S.P. Shillong from 1969 to 1972, when Shillong was the capital of undivided Assam. He was a very demanding chief but one who got the loyalty of his juniors without asking for it.

He led a full and eventful life and he has gone to the eternal rest after completing a long and distinguished innings. He has also sired a very talented family which will be his enduring legacy.

My wife Patricia joins me in extending to the entire family our very sincere condolences. Shri Dey has left behind a void which cannot be filled.

With kind regards,

Yours sincerely

Chi...

TRIBUTES

Lala B.K. Dey: An Old-World Leader

Herminder Gill

My first meeting with Mr Lala B.K. Dey was at Dergaon, during a visit by the Governor. My husband, K.P.S. Gill, was the Additional Superintendent of Police at Dibrugarh. I was a new bride and had recently arrived in Assam after our marriage. I remember the Governor was to attend a police meet at Dergaon, a few hours' drive from Dibrugarh. As he was coming with his family, I recall Mrs Rahman, DIG's wife asked me to look after the Governor's daughter, who turned out to be a fellow Bedean (from St. Bedes College, Shimla) like I was!

It was here that I was introduced to Mr Dey. Our first encounter was brief and superficial, but his impact on me was immediate. Mr Dey was personable, handsome with a great sense of style and, most importantly, a thorough gentleman, considerate, courteous, tremendously at ease. Over time, we would grow much closer to him and his family, but this first impression was only to be reinforced with every meeting and interaction.

Through his life, my husband found few individuals who he frankly and openly admitted an admiration for, and Mr Dey was one among this very small number. Mr Gill often spoke about Mr Dey's leadership, his penchant, at once, for military discipline (owing to his army background) and for compassion towards subordinates, as well as, crucially, his capacity for clear articulation of commands and the unambiguous delegation of authority.

In the years that Mr Dey was the Inspector General of Police (then the highest rank in the State Police Force), first of undivided Assam, and then of Assam after full statehood was granted to Meghalaya in 1972, the state saw frequent and widespread disturbances, particularly as a result of the anti-outsider movement. Mr Dey came to rely increasingly on my husband to handle the most troubling of situations, and always trusted him implicitly, giving him complete independence to respond as he thought best to the crises on the ground. It was a pattern of operation that allowed two strong personalities to interact without friction, and to produce extraordinary results in very difficult times.

After my husband passed away in May 2017, a number of officers who had served with him in Assam would drop in and recount those times they had spent with him. It was lovely going down the memory lane, reliving an astonishing period of upheavals in Assam, punctuated with some very warm recollections of times spent together. One such conversation was with Anil Chowdhury, who had joined the Assam cadre as a young Additional Superintendent of Police in 1971, and reported to his IG, Mr Dey, at Shillong. Anil recalls, 'I was received by the IGP in his office with warmth and great courtesy. Normally, all newly inducted IPS officers were sent to the State Police Training School at Ri-Bhoi for a stint, but Mr Dey told me that I would 'train' on the job, under his most dynamic and effective District Police Chief, K.P.S. Gill, at Guwahati. I was to learn practical policing from him: how to handle rioting, crime, and law and order situations. He'll teach you everything, he said, he's the best.'

The SP's Bungalow in Guwahati was a legendary residence, an immense property situated on the banks of the Brahmaputra.

A very beautiful bungalow, built in the traditional Ahom style, with a thatched roof, with acres of exquisitely cultivated land all around. The rear veranda opened out onto this amazing vista of the Brahmaputra, with the temple island of Umananda just across, in the middle of the river. It was almost like having the Brahmaputra flowing through our backyard. It was an amazing sight, this immense, majestic river flowing by. Acres of gardens, ancient trees, and a pukhri—a pond—blooming with lotus flowers. It was a residence fit for a king, and rumour has it that it had at one time been a royal residence.

When Anil Chowdhury joined duties at Guwahati, there was no suitable residence for him. Anil recalls, 'There was no house. I was running from Circuit House to Railway House to the PWD Guest House, managing as best I could.' Mr Gill decided an appropriate residence was needed immediately. An area on one side of the sprawling grounds of the SP's Bungalow was earmarked for the construction of a cottage. By the time this was ready, however, Anil had been transferred out of Guwahati.

Assam's capital was shifted from Shillong to Guwahati (technically to Dispur) in January 1972, and with it, the IG's office and residence. Guwahati was a tiny little town at that time, and Dispur little more than a stretch of farmland under cultivation. There was no suitable accommodation for the IG and the natural expectation was that the best residence available for the police, the SP's Bungalow, would be most suitable for the IG. But Mr Dey insisted he 'did not wish to disturb the SP's Bungalow,' and very graciously chose to live in the cottage constructed for the ASP, Anil Chowdhury! The cottage was, of course, enlarged and made more suitable for the IG and his family, but I cannot imagine such generosity of spirit and such a lack of concern for rank, status and pelf in any one of the hundreds of officers I have met and interacted with since!

It was after Mr Dey moved into the cottage on the SP's Bungalow compound that the relationship between his family and ours became very close. Mr Dey was already very fond of my husband as an officer and as a man, and trusted him with the most difficult jobs. They also got along very well because they shared a deep interest in literature and poetry. Mr Dey was a very educated, erudite man. He was an old-world gentleman, civilized, cultured, with a great love for horses and riding, and like my husband, had a tremendous fondness for dogs. Our families would often spend long evenings together either at his residence or ours, discussing literature, music, films. Our children spent a lot of time with each other. When Mr Dey travelled out of town, he would leave his family in my husband's care.

Mr Dey's faith in my husband, however, already went back several years by this time. They worked closely together when my husband was SP Shillong (technically SP, United Khasi and Jaintia Hills in undivided Assam) between 1965 and 1967, when intense political activity and a frequent threat of 'direct action' for a separate Hill State prevailed. A political movement for a separate Hill State had been ongoing since the mid-1950s, but it intensified after 1960, when the Assam Government announced a new 'language policy' which made Assamese the official language of the state—a decision that was seen by the tribal people of the Hill Areas as an assault on their culture. By and large, however, the Hill State movement remained off the streets and was non-violent. The movement did briefly launch an agitation in 1968, when 'non-violent direct action' was initiated.

But the troubles in Shillong and the wider hill region never escalated into a major crisis and were largely managed politically by the Centre. As a result, when the anti-outsider movement was launched in the plain areas of United Assam in 1969, Mr Dey needed a reliable trouble shooter. He decided to send my husband down as SP Guwahati, and from this point on, it was a rolling crisis. As P.V. Sumant, one of the ASPs who worked with my husband at this time (and who later retired after serving as the Director General of Police, Assam), recalled, 'Rioting used to start in August and end in October, till 1979. Then it started and never ended.' Mr Dey would frequently come to Guwahati from Shillong to review the situation, and an increasingly close working relationship emerged in which, I recall, my husband appreciated the clarity of instructions he received and the degree of autonomy he enjoyed under the IG's command.

Mr Dey was also old school as far as crime and investigation were concerned. He was a stickler for the integrity of process and, as P.C. Sharma, another of my husband's ASPs at that time (and who eventually retired as Director, Central Bureau of Investigation), 'insisted on correct reporting in crime situations. Police reports were often ambiguous, but he always insisted on short, crisp and accurate reports.' This was another point on which there was a meeting of minds with my husband, who tended to be direct and brief in his communications, and expected a similar dependability and brevity from his subordinates.

Mr Dey was also exceptional in his concern for the rank and file of the Force. He did a lot of work in the Police Reserves, ensuring that his men and their families were well looked after, and this, again, was a trait he shared with my husband, who always insisted that the quality of command could be judged by the welfare of the lowest ranks.

There were lovely times together in Guwahati, till Mr

Dey retired in 1975. There were picnics together, family trips to Manas, and to the Daranga Mela on the border of Bhutan, where Bhutia dogs were sold, and we returned with little puppies, who long served as living reminders of those beautiful days and years. Mr Dey had a strong sense of family, and was very fond of children. Mrs Dey was a wonderful lady, very strong and dignified. I admired her a great deal and she was extremely fond of me. She belonged to a very prominent family of Meghalaya, and Mrs and Mr Dey would shuttle between Guwahati and the family's properties in Shillong. Mr Dey would always remember my daughter's favourite pastries, and bring a box down from Mahari's Bakery in Shillong. Mrs and Mr Dey were also perfect hosts, and we were often welcomed at their farmhouse in Shillong.

K.P.S. Gill, I and my family remember Lala Dey and Mrs Dey with great affection and fondness. Mr Dey was a man with an aura around him, and the police fraternity in Assam, and particularly the young officers, looked up to him. My husband was fortunate to have served under such a gracious, sage and sophisticated commander in the early stages of his career. He belonged to a rare breed even in his age; such men can no longer be found.

'What a Man!' George Bernard Shaw

Sudipta Bhattacharjee

Resident Editor (Northeast)
The Telegraph, June 2020

My husband Subir was posted in Shillong for three years from 1992. I took a transfer from Kolkata as senior correspondent of *The Telegraph* during that period—our first stay outside the city of our birth. We landed amid ethnic riots and stayed in a house at Laban belonging to the genial Winnie Kharkongor. Much to our delight and good fortune, we were befriended by our wonderful neighbour, Pradip Kumar Dey Chowdhury, who took us under his wing and made our stay utterly memorable.

Uncle Pradip, as we called him, showed us Shillong and its inhabitants so intimately that we fell in love with the abode of clouds and its people. One of the first families he took us to visit was that of his cousin, Lala B.K. Dey, in Lower Mawprem, on a Sunday morning. It was a day that is etched indelibly in our mind's eye. Lala Dey and his wife extended their love for Uncle to us with such magnanimity and benevolence that we were included in all family gatherings during the rest of our stay.

When we entered the gates of Lakyrsiew, my first thought was of beholding a fairytale setting, a tree-lined driveway, a beautiful house with gables, horses grazing in the distance, the green hills as a backdrop. A tall, resplendent gentleman came out and greeted Uncle warmly. We had been told about Lala B.K. Dey's illustrious career in the police force of Assam and his youthful adventures, but nothing had prepared us for the enormity of his sheer presence. Uncle Pradip introduced us and Lala Dey immediately made us feel at home with his eloquence and conversational skills. He spoke Bengali (including Sylheti), Khasi and English in our presence with perfect diction and accent. On a later occasion, he quipped that he 'preferred the Queen's English' to the medley we hear all around. In all my life, I am yet to meet anyone to match his towering personality.

He was the first person who prodded in me a quest for identity. 'What are your roots?' he asked me in a booming voice. Till that moment, it was a subject my youthful self had not bothered with at all. 'Do you know where your ancestors came from?' he queried. I could trace my family tree up to my grandfather, no further. 'Know the value of your roots,' he advised gently. 'Try to find out.' To think this stress on legacy data came decades before the current imbroglio over the Citizenship (Amendment) Act!

Lala Dey showed us around his sprawling garden, his beloved horses, the pear trees, the cattle shed, till his lovely wife, Lisimon Sawian, came out in her wheelchair to greet us just as warmly. It was a winter's day, the dry pine cones crackled in the hearth, creating an ambience that is imprinted in our memory.

Refreshments were served in a delightful array: delicious sandwiches, cakes, delicacies and tea. We warmed to both of them and could understand why Uncle Pradip revered and loved Lala and his wife so much.

On Bengali New Year's Day the following year, Lala Dey invited us to his lovely home for a sumptuous Bengali lunch. As my husband was at work, Uncle Pradip took me to Lower Mawprem.

Lala Dey stood outside to greet us, clad in dhoti-punjabi, the perfect Bangali bhadralok greeting his guests with a 'namaskar.'

We visited Lakyrsiew several times during our stay, our bond with Lala Dey and his wife growing stronger with each meeting. We were introduced to their wonderful children: Bijoya, Bijon, Prabhat, Parvati and Nayantara on various occasions; they and their families are precious friends to this day.

In 1995, we returned to Kolkata. When Lala Dey passed away, Bijon wrote a heartwarming tribute that *The Telegraph* was privileged to publish. I visited Meghalaya soon thereafter, while Uncle Pradip was still there. He insisted that I visit Lala Dey's house and meet Aunty Lisimon. Ever the gracious hostess, she told me, 'I am so happy you have come. I would have been hurt and disappointed if I heard you had visited Shillong, however briefly, and not met me.' I could have hugged her joyfully for exuding such warmth.

That was my last visit to Lakyrsiew. As we left the gates, I felt the absence of Lala Dey like a huge void. It was an irrevocable loss that Uncle Pradip felt till his last breath in a Kolkata hospital. I know they are united joyously in the hereafter and chatting by the hearth in heaven, just like in the old days in Shillong, clinking their glasses and raising a toast.

Boromama

Monica Sen Saha

A man who stood head and shoulders above others, he was held in great esteem. His intelligence, ethics, integrity and candour plus his charm and humour and his laugh attracted all who met him.

He grew up in an austere household where good food, good education and family responsibility were the foundations. His parents were very young when they relocated from Sylhet to Shillong pre-partition. My grandfather, having recently lost his father and their property in Sylhet, had started a law practice and, apart from his wife and children, had to support many dependants. Boromama, as the eldest son, was raised in my grandfather Lala Bijoy Kumar Dey's mould as a Hindu patriarch in all the best connotations of the word.

Boromama and my mother Bina were the eldest two out of seven children. Both were much alike… charismatic, confident, assertive, loving and fierce, strongly imbued with responsibility towards family. They loved, respected and admired each other yet there was a strong rivalry between them. As a child, I would listen to their scathing arguments and I would feel my mother was very brave to face the powerhouse that was Boromama. She was often called to settle family disputes and mitigate his wrath, which often ended in their ability to overcome anger and find humour. The family dynamics of the Deys were volatile and very interesting.

Towards the end of his life, Boromama was admitted to Gangaram Hospital in Delhi, seriously ill. I happened to visit the city at that time and went to see him with my husband and cousin Meenakshi, 'Mimi'. He was lying down with headphones on, eyes closed listening to Beethoven's 5th. Hearing my voice, his eyes opened and smiled and he said, 'So you've come.' On seeing Mimi beside me, he charged her with neglecting him. She protested she had come to see him. It never paid to be submissive, he liked us to show 'spirit'. He ordered that I cook for him some 'edible' food. There was, surprisingly, a small kitchen set up in the alcove of his hospital room, his orderly in attendance. Boromama told me that Ronjona, a cousin, had disappeared. She was bringing him fish curry till she was told it was not permitted in his diet. She told me later that her coming empty-handed disappointed him which she could not bear. Mimi was sent off to get provisions. There was a call from Shillong. Boroma spoke to Lisimon Maima and complained 'They are not feeding me properly. Oongoo is cooking for me.' Through all this, his daughters Bijoya and Parvati sat quietly, watching this little drama unfold, probably happy to be temporarily out of the line of fire. Boromama looked at me and said 'Thank God you have your father's nose and not your mother's!'

The provisions arrived, brought by a harassed Mimi. The shops were largely shut and she had had to drive around to get all the items. The orderly was told to watch and learn so as to be able to duplicate what I was making and I was told to hurry up! The food was made with many urgings. Since I was not too confident of the outcome, I decided we should leave and worried that the expectation was tiring him out.

As I was saying goodbye, Boromama asked me to bend down and kissed me on both cheeks. He closed his eyes and said, 'one kiss for your father and one for your mother!' This was the last time I saw him.

Boromama's wife, Lisimon Maima was a lady of tremendous strength and grace. Paralyzed for decades by arthritis, her will power, steady presence and understanding was his backbone and control. Although there were occasions when she would ask my mother to referee!

Boromama had an illustrious career in the British Army and then the police, leaving his stamp on both services as well as on the civilian community in which he lived. Much is and will be written on those aspects of his life, achievements and on his multifaceted personality. I can write about him as my beloved, feared and admired uncle who set such high standards.

As children, visiting my grandparents' home in Shillong,

where we were born and grew up, was the highlight of our lives. It was Boromama who arranged for our travel up from Guwahati. He would make sure the driver had a full jerrican of water in the boot, as he knew that I could not withstand the winding hill road and would require a wash down at least once in the journey. He would declare that only milk from his dairy and Nongpo bananas could rid us of our city pallor. He knew my sister Milonee and his son Bijon were sneaking off with his jeep to practice driving. He would berate them and the shivering driver, but he never really put a stop to their ambitions.

When my father died, we had gone to Hardwar to perform his last rites. Boromama and Lisimon Maima, who were visiting Bijoya in Dehradun, were present and supported my mother, sister and I through this difficult time. He was asked to perform the Kanyadaan when I got married in Kolkata some years later. He was unwell, so another uncle was asked to step in. The day before the wedding, he arrived from Shillong, accompanied by the manager of his dairy farm. I got married with two uncles taking on my father's duty. He told my mother he felt I needed him to take on this parental duty. I married a widower with two young girls. He told me sternly my duty henceforth would be to 'cherish' my daughters as they were now my responsibility.

A man with many demands on his time and attention, he gave us, his nieces and nephews an abundance of attention and affection. I am truly fortunate and privileged to have him as my role model, so much affection and care, for a large part of my life. How many have had the luck to have a Boromama such as he?

When I think of him, which is often, my favorite image is of him magnificentonabig horse accompanied by his rather ferocious German Shepherd Bagha, riding up to the front verandah of my grandparents' home, where we would all be lined up waiting for his daily morning visit to see his parents.

Me (extreme right) with Boromama (1967)

Remembering Lala Sahib

Raj Deo Rai

Narrated to Ms Rinku Rai
10 July 2020

I am Raj Deo Rai, residing at 3½ Mile Upper Shillong since 1971, in Lala Sahib's estate.

He was and is my favourite person, someone I admired and respected the most. Not because he was a man of position but because of the love and affection he showed towards me and my family members. Words are less for me to describe him for he never made me feel the absence of my parents.

The first time my father, the late Shree Ram Deo Rai, came to Shillong with the purpose of starting a small business, it was Lala Sahib who supported him by gifting him some cows. It was a blessing from him that though being unknown to the new place, he lived comfortably and carried on his business. Lala Sahib at first gave us a space at his dairy farm at Lower Mawprem and later shifted us to 3½ Mile, Upper Shillong.

He was very fond of horses and loved riding. He spent most of his leisure time doing that. The queen of Silchar (Kachari Road) once gifted him a female horse, whom he named 'Tari'. Later he purchased one female horse from Markasa and one male horse from Kynshi and continued the process of rearing horses throughout his life. Whenever he got to know about horses being reared at any place, he was sure to go and look for them. I would always accompany him. He also never missed horse racing programmes at any place.

I followed him to many places across India and to the remotest places in Meghalaya. Wherever he visited, he earned great respect and love from people. It was through him that I was connected to many other respected persons. He inspired me a lot and taught me great values of life—like how to respect people, listen to their opinions, care for their opinions, to be bold and at the same time to be humble and kind towards others.

I feel so privileged to have known him and worked with him. I must say that I owe my identity to him and I am thankful to this great leader for making my life significant.

Lala B.K. Dey Esqr.

Asish Kumar Chowdhuri (Babloo)

Lala Bimalendu Kumar Dey was an officer who was commissioned into the Royal Indian Artillery during the Great War. Subsequently, post India's independence, he joined the Indian Police Service and rose to its top position.

From his childhood, he was very closely rooted to my father Amulya Bhusan Chowdhuri, a bureaucrat in the undivided state of Assam. I recall a family story that he wrote most of his undergraduate examination papers when he stayed in our house in Shillong in the latter part of the 1930s. My father had given him a room in the adjoining cottage to study for his exams.

Benu Kaka, as I called him, was a man of all seasons. He was a stalwart in every sense, both physically and mentally. He had a passion for horses and was a competent rider. He was also a well-read man, kind, broadminded and at the same time, a very strict disciplinarian.

He was extremely fond of me, and I in turn was very appreciative and an admirer of him. Our holiday in Shillong was never complete without a visit to Umsohsun, and later, the Manor house he built within the dairy farm in Lower Mawprem. Quite coincidentally, Benu Kaka had known my in-laws and Krishna my wife as a child when he was posted in Upper Assam in the mid-1950s.

Krishna and I would always look forward to his visits to us when he would tour the tea growing areas of Upper Assam. We used to enjoy the messages that would filter in from the local police station on the progress of his journey to our home. It was because he never wanted to keep us waiting in anticipation of his arrival—a fine trait of a gentleman of yore.

A few years back, I, along with my brother, sister and brother-in-law, had taken a nostalgic trip to our ancestral landed property in the vicinity of Sylhet. Interestingly, adjoining our property was a tea factory where I met a person related to Benu Kaka from his maternal side. The family had stayed back in East Bengal after Partition.

There is no end to reminiscing. On one occasion, I had pinched a long weekend to Shillong to visit my mother. To my horror, an Assam Bandh was declared by certain groups of agitators in the Brahmaputra valley, and I was truly in a fix. I rushed to Benu Kaka, who was then the police chief of undivided Assam. In his imitable way, he sat me down and told me to relax. He penned down a few lines addressed to the Superintendents of Police of Kamrup, Nowgong,

Sibsagar and Dibrugarh districts to ensure a safe passage to my destination.

Such was the versatility of the man.

Benuda

Joyabrata Narayan Deb Choudhury

Since our childhood, Shillong, Meghalya has been a very special and cool place for our holidays. We visited our cousin Benuda's home many times, with or without our late father, Jitendra Narayan Deb Choudhury. We would look forward to and dream of our Shillong visits. Our beloved 'Benuda', who was the IGP of Assam, was well known to all as Lala B.K. Dey. He was our first cousin. Our father, the late Advocate Jitendra Narayan Deb Choudhury, was his eldest maternal uncle. He had a very cordial relationship with our father. During the liberation war of Bangladesh, we remembered Benuda's great support when we shifted to India. We were forced to leave East Bengal and take shelter in India in a helpless condition. It was Benuda who extended all support and help to us. It would have been impossible and very difficult for us to stay in a foreign land without his help and support.

My father, J.N. Deb Choudhury, was a renowned lawyer in Bangladesh, and he was also a very social, strong and organized person. During that time, there were no cell phones, no internet but we kept in regular contact with our family members in Bangladesh and in India by handwritten letters. My father was born and raised in a large and wealthy family. Our grandfather, the late Joy Narayan Deb Choudhury, was also a renowned lawyer. After nine daughters were born to him, both my grandparents went to Kamakhya Mandir in Gauhati, Assam for seeking the goddess' blessing for a son. As we know, my father was born and he was given the name 'Kamakhya'. After that, our uncle Jnanendra Narayan was born. When our grandfather passed away, my father was a law student at Calcutta University. He was suddenly faced with very difficult times for completing his law study, and at the same time, he needed to arrange for his sister's wedding. My father returned to Sylhet and started his law practice. In 1965, many Hindu families moved to India but we remained in Sylhet.

After Bangladesh attained its independence, Benuda brought our grandmother, Tripura Sundori, back to our home at Fenchuganj in Bangladesh—I think it was sometime in 1972. Our father started rebuilding our house, office, and the tea garden which were partially or completely destroyed. He restarted his law practice. After over fifty years as a lawyer, our father passed away in 1995 when he was 85. He established his name by setting up an institute of law, called J.N. Deb Advocate and Associates.

We are three brothers and one sister. Our Mother Khushi Rani Choudhury (81) is living in our family home in Kastoghor, Sylhet. She remembers Shillong very fondly, especially Lismon Boudi. My elder brother, Advocate Jyotirmoy, became a judge at the High Court of Dhaka, Bangladesh in 2014. But unfortunately, he died of colon cancer at the very young age of fifty-two years. I and my brother are presently living in Canada, and our only sister is living in Dhaka. To this day, we are managing our tea estate in Fenchuganj, Sylhet. My brother and I visit Sylhet twice a year.

Thanks to Jayantada, our first paternal cousin, I could communicate with Bijoya after a long time.

We will always remember Benuda and his entire family with much gratitude and affection. The holidays in Shillong are always talked about with great fondness, and we remember how we used to long with all our hearts for the time when we could escape from the heat in Sylhet to Benuda's home in Shillong.

Riding with Lala Dey

Jyoti Jafa

When we first met, Lala B.K. Dey was still the IGP of Assam, and I just a junior officer's wife who had left the Foreign Service and begun writing books. But real horse people have a bond transcending gender, age, and every hierarchy thanks to their passion, these amazing animals and keeping fast-disappearing equestrian skills alive.

Coming from a very horsey Rajput background, I always sought opportunities for riding. Lala Dey offered them by including our family in that small group helping to keep some police horses, once used for touring remote interiors, well exercised. And as a perfect Bengali aristocrat, Lala Dey allotted me his own favourite mount, Isabelle, a perfectly trained and beautiful thoroughbred.

However, this gracious gentleman had one inflexible rule: 'People riding with me must wear protective headgear, and never mind your views about the Queen of England riding around Windsor wearing just a headscarf since childhood!'

A great rider and animal lover, Lala Dey often spoke about Shillong's potential for pony trekking and horse safari. He also regretted the shutting down of its British era polo club and racecourse, which used to attract so many riders, players, and visitors from all over eastern India. But even during the 1970s and 80s, riding through the unspoilt Khasi countryside with its green hills and valleys, pine and bamboo forest, waterfalls, streams and charming tribal villages surrounded by fruit gardens and flowers, was such a great pleasure.

Except once, when my husband Hari, the newly appointed DC Khasi Hills, suggested we take a short cut from the Laitkor peak after an exhausting cross-country ride. Lala Dey and his son Bijon—also an IPS officer—were used to the risks involved. And I knew my mount Isabella could take anything in her stride.

As we began descending, I lost a stirrup. No sooner was this rectified than the wonder horse Isabella turned sharply off that steep, narrow trek, coming to a dead halt. Then, I went flying over her head as my saddle came off. And largely thanks to her horse-sense plus Lala Dey's hardhat policy, I came off unhurt that day on that hillside more suitable for rock climbing than pony-trekking.

Despite being the oldest person there, Lala Dey quickly dismounted to help me up with some morale boosting words: 'Even the best of riders take tumbles when their saddles come off.'

With a hospitable and lively family, Lala Dey liked taking us home for after-ride breakfast or high tea. But on an unforgettable day during the infamous anti-outsider violence in Shillong, he invited us instead to the Circuit House after our ride to meet a visiting retired colleague, now settled abroad. While we sat listening to them discussing about those good old days when this was such a peaceful place, the air raid sirens installed there during the Bangladesh War began blaring.

Thoroughly spooked, those supposedly well-trained horses used for crowd control bolted across the terraced garden, jumping every hurdle, including our breakfast table. And galloped off down the tarmac road, going towards the busy bazaar.

But Lala Dey retained his usual sangfroid. 'Where can they go?' he asked, commandeering the nearest official jeep to track them down.

He soon found those horses entertaining a growing crowd while foraging for their own breakfast from some Khasi Kong's vegetable stalls!

Lala B.K. Dey

Deepak Narain Dutt IPS (Retd.)

By the time I had joined the service in the year 1971 and been attached to the IGP's office in the then Assam Capital in Shillong, the name of Lala Bimalendu Kumar Dey (more popularly known as Lala B.K. Dey) was a name that evoked awe and not a little trepidation. This reputation was well-earned no doubt owing largely to his magnetic personality and no-nonsense attitude but when I first went to formally call on him in his office chamber, under that veneer, he presented a side of himself which to a young officer fresh out of training, was both a relief and a revelation. The great man, after the initial formalities, made enquiries about my accommodation and immediately ordered that I be allotted a vehicle and a batman and to report to the IGP's office everyday for my various attachments with sundry officers. I had my work cut out! That first encounter with him, though brief, left a deep impression on a young mind that was longing to be a part of the police fraternity.

A quaint and delightful aspect to this great man's personality was his love of horses and it was indeed magical to see him come to office in full uniform astride one, with a riding crop hanging loosely from one hand! Today, one wonders what happened to all his beloved steeds!

Lala B.K. Dey was indeed the quintessential policeman, solidly built with strong features and with a steady unwavering gaze that seemed to size me up from head to toe, with just a hint of a smile hovering around his mouth. If a trainee police officer was looking for a role model, then Lala B.K. Dey was the ideal example of a tough professional whose integrity and work ethics were beyond question.

On the occasion of his centenary year, I pay my respectful homage to the memory of a veritable icon, a conscientious professional, and above all, a good human being.

The Lone Horseman

Brigadier Amlan Pratap Datta

For months before he left us, he was restricted to limited physical activity. Having known him for his love of horses and horsemanship, in my mind's eye, I see him on horseback, slowly cantering over the horizon into eternity.

He left us, never to return, on 10th July 2001. Time has healed the pain of loss that his dear ones felt on his demise but memories of all that was remarkable in him come tumbling back to remind us of those great days when he was in his prime.

We recall everything with a sense of joy. I for one would like to believe that he rode out of life like the gallant mounted warrior that he always was.

He enjoyed riding on the various rides made for horsemen like the Laitkor Ride, Maupat Ride and many more which have fallen into disuse.

I first met him at Silchar in December 1948 where he

was posted as Superintendent of Police when my father was carrying out land survey of the district. The first impression he left was that of a very well turned-out officer with a soldierly bearing and an awe-inspiring presence.

His demeanor prompted men to follow him. Calm in crisis and decisive in action, he was an asset to the Assam Police who will always remember him for this.

He was my mother's cousin and a maternal uncle to us.

In the Pathariya Reserve forest, the Pakistani Rangers had occupied a part of the forest. Lala B.K. Dey put in a lightning attack with whatever troops he had. In this action, he earned fame for the Assam Police and made a name for himself as a battle-hardened leader of men.

Because he had led from the front, they were ready to follow him be it to hell and back. The Pathariya assault was the defining moment of Lala B.K. Dey's career. He came to be known as a daring and ferocious officer who was willing to take the battle to the enemy whatever be the odds.

Whatever he did was always done in a big way. He loved animals and kept about a dozen dogs around his premises. He rode ponies and kept about ten animals in his stable. His herd of cattle, a barn full of about thirty heads of milking cows, loved him as much as he loved them. When he got out of his house, the dogs would bark a welcome and as he crossed the stable, the ponies would neigh. When he reached the barn, the cows would moo in unison. He was at his best in his world of animals.

Benu Mama had a degree of flamboyance built in his

character. He lived life large and largess stood out when anyone came to him for help. In deserving cases, he extended all out assistance.

As a leader, he could be compared with Rhett Butler of Margaret Mitchell's *Gone with the Wind* or the protagonist of Mario Puzo's *The Godfather* or any of Earnest Hemingway's male heroes. However, he was his own man not to be typecast with any fictional characters.

Topped off by all his fine manly qualities was a volcanic temper which occasionally erupted leaving him spewing fire and brimstone which made him an even more colourful character. His gentle wife often intervened to help him cool off.

Ability to organize events on a large scale was one of his special traits. Be it a Horse Show or a Ceremonial Parade or the largest wedding ever held in Shillong...when his daughters were wed. Every detail was gone into and nothing was left to chance. Everything went off with clockwork precision. He did things in style and delivered with elan.

After a visit to Benu Mama, my son then only ten years old, exclaimed. 'Daddy, your uncle is a lion.' After a few days, he rang me up and wanted an appointment with the army dentist. I fixed it up but as he was having high blood pressure, he had to be admitted in the Military Hospital and medicated till his blood pressure came within permissible limits. I escorted him to the Surgery and he requested the dentist to permit me to remain in the Surgery. He was feeling apprehensive. So was the dentist who was visibly overawed by his personality. As soon as he was seated in the dental chair, he took a firm grip of my right hand with the pressure increasing with each move the dentist made. With a sudden flick of his wrist, the dental surgeon had the decaying tooth out. Benu Mama was without his leonine mantle. As soon as the extraction was over, he released his vice-like grip on my hand, which had turned blue and was soon himself again. That was the only time in life I saw Benu Mama scared of anything and the dentist who was mortally scared of his wrath was much relieved to see him in good humour.

Tribute to Parad Mawprem

Colonel Brijesh Singh Sawian
1/3 Gorkha Rifles

Happy to know that a book will be out soon on Parad Benu (Late Shri Lala B.K. Dey). I was so proud to learn that Parad was a Gunner (Corps of Artillery), before joining the IPS. I have such fond memories of him as we would visit him and Meirad Li often in their estate in Mawprem. Parad shared a great bond with my father late Lt Col Randhir Singh Rawat. My father respected him immensely for his sense of duty, discipline and his personality and his views which were unbiased to any creed and culture. Parad respected people for their character and deeds and did not believe in any caste and class distinction. My parents and grandparents would always talk of his admirable trait of being comfortable with all the members of the family in Shillong and his kindness and generosity.

As a child, I used to be very excited whenever a plan was

made to go to Mawprem. I can proudly say that I was one of his favourites as I knew riding—a sport I had mastered in Nagaland where my dad was posted. I was allowed to ride his horses. I remember a sprightly mare, Champa.

A high tea would follow. We children sat apart which was perfect for me as I could eat and chatter to my heart's content! Meirad Li and Parad Benu were excellent hosts and would always remember their guests' favourites. So there would be toast and butter, Mahari cookies (mixed cakes as they were called) and chicken patties for all of us and rosgullas from Delhi Mistan of course and special payash made for my mother. Parad would personally see that we eat to our hearts' content.

I remember his firm handshake followed by an affectionate pat on the back as we left and bid good bye.

These are the precious memories I have of an unforgettable grand uncle and a great man. Respect!

Tribute to Bah Benu

Sarahline Tham

Jaïaw Langsning
24th August 2020

It was during the late 1940s, after my father Jor Manik Sing Syiem joined the Bar that we became associated with Bah Benu's father, Lala Bijoy Kumar Dey and his family.

Lala Bimalendu Kumar Dey, Bah Benu as he was known to us, lived in a very pretty house at Jaïaw Pdeng, Main Road and Bah Benu's mother would often sit in the verandah reading a book.

Later, when Bah Benu married Kong Lisimon Sawian and they moved to Mawprem, I have vivid memories of him riding his horse, crossing the small bylane by our house at Jaïaw Langsning towards the Jaïaw Main Road looking ever so grand. What impressed me the most was that he always wore a smile on his face, greeting us youngsters in his chaste Sohra accent.

Both he and his wife came to my wedding on 2nd November 1965 and along with the gift, they sent me fresh slipper orchids for my bouquet from their garden, in the morning of the wedding.

My last recollection of Lala B.K. Dey was when he came home, on the eve of my father's funeral in January 1999. He gently removed his cap as he stood by the coffin, silently, to pay his last respects.

Remembering Uncle Lala

Rashid Kidwai

Uncle Lala and my father, the late A.N. Kidwai, worked very closely together. He, as the Inspector General of Police (in those days, you did not have a Director General of Police, the IGP was the head of the State Police Force) and my father was the Chief Secretary in undivided Assam. They were in-charge during very tumultuous times such as the Chinese aggression in 1962, the war with Pakistan in 1965, the Naga Accord, the language riots, the Lushai Hills problems, the anti-Bengali/Marwari and Nepali stirs, and many more.

They had a great working relationship and a high regard and respect for each other. Apart from the official relationship, there was also a very warm personal relationship where in addition to the official functions, the families would often call on each other. I remember their lovely home in Umsohsun and later after uncle's retirement, their other lovely home at Lower Mawprem with the Bishop and Bidon Falls just behind, where we also had some enjoyable times.

We used to hear about Uncle Lala and how well he was respected by the force from more junior officers like Mr Chittaranjan, who was the Superintendent of Police of the then United Khasi and Jaintia Hills with its headquarter in Shillong, and also from a host of other people like Charlie Gafoor and Bill Richmond about what an upright gentleman Uncle Lala was and the values he maintained and encouraged his junior officers to adopt.

Our mothers were also good friends and enjoyed meeting apart from their social work initiatives.

We've been family friends for three generations, Bijon, Prabhat and I were in the same class in St. Edmunds and Bijon, and I went on to St. Stephen's for three years and Prabhat to the Delhi School of Architecture. Bijoya and Parvati studied for their undergraduate degree at the Lady Shri Ram College in New Delhi. We continued with our ties and friendship through our days in university and we have remained in touch till today despite us being in different ends of the country. Our children too are friends.

Bijon and I have taken many road trips together as both of us enjoy the feeling of liberty that the highway provides. Both of us participated in the 2nd Asian Highway Rally from Tehran to Dhaka in 1970. It was only Uncle Lala and my father who gave us the permission. Though a lot of friends wanted to join us, it was Bunny (A.P. Singh who went on to head the CBI) who joined us in Kabul. Our parents encouraged and helped us with many of our adventures.

I have some very fond memories of Uncle and Aunty.

Lala B.K. Dey: A Wonderful Soul and Animal Lover

Dr Basana Ranjan Halder

Guwahati

This is with reference to the article authored by Sameer Sohliya which was published in the esteemed weekly, *The Sentinel Melange* on 30th September 2012.

The article referred to Lala B.K. Dey, former Police Chief of undivided Assam and a photograph of his two sons, Bijon Sawian with his brother and their horses. It also mentioned, 'His father's horses can still be seen grazing on the sprawling lawns and gardens of the family home in Mawprem.'

This leads me to reminisce about my association with a wonderful soul and an avid animal lover. When Lala B.K. Dey was posted in Guwahati (1964-1969), I had the opportunity to become acquainted with him because, besides his love for horses, he was an avid animal lover and raised a beautiful dairy herd at his Mawprem home.

He often visited me and was eager to utilize my services as an Animal Health specialist (in the Animal Husbandry and Veterinary Department of Assam) and desired my regular visit to Mawprem for regular health check-ups of his dairy herd and horses.

He also often sought technical advice for the health and care of the pets he was very much involved with.

On my visits, I was always warmly received by him and his wife, and in my routine inspection of his dairy sheds, I would find him in breeches and gum boots. What impressed me was his great love for each and every milch cow, which he knew by name (given by him), and the way he would treat them, which was lovingly reciprocated by the animals.

Lala B.K. Dey was also instrumental in raising the Mounted Squad of Assam Police and he took my help while visiting the Army Stud Farm at Hosiarpur to pick healthy and sound horses for the police squad.

The first batch of horses for the mounted police was kept in my custody at the Animal Health Centre at Khanapara for quarantine, blood tests and immunization on their arrival.

The article helped me to recall those eventful days and my admiration for Lala B.K. Dey.

Grand Old Man of the Police Force

Sanjay Sharma

The Sentinel, Dated the 8th of May, 1988

If there is a grand old man of the police force, it is Lala B.K. Dey. When I made telephonic contact with him and told him that I was interested in doing a personal sketch of him, the two words that he uttered by way of expression were 'Good God!' He, nonetheless, condescended to grant me an interview over breakfast the next morning, and so it was that I made my hesitant way to his bungalow of which, apart from the fact that it was located in Mawprem, Shillong, I knew practically nothing. It was neither a long search, nor an unfructuous one. He is popularly known to the locals as IG Saheb or Bah Benu, and I had no difficulty in locating his house.

I met him while he was on his way to visit his one-month-old granddaughter, whom he dotes on. He was not irritated at my interruption of his constitutional nor at my intrusion of his privacy. He led me instead to his bungalow nearby where whilst enjoying the view of the hills from his morning room, I was transported into the past.

The eldest son of an illustrious lawyer from Sylhet who has chosen to settle in Shillong, Lala B.K. Dey was educated while at school at St. Edmunds', Shillong. On completing his Senior Cambridge, he issued notice to his father that if he was to go on to college, it would be at Calcutta or nowhere. Being the eldest son, his father was rather indulgent of him and time soon saw the young B.K. Dey on his way to Calcutta of which he had heard so much. He was sixteen at the time. But with the characteristics of an infatuation, the novelty of the big city soon wore thin and he was yearning to be back in Shillong. Came the Puja holidays and once home, he refused to return to Calcutta. The prodigal was admitted into the same institution he had left not long before and thus completed his graduation.

'Somewhere at the back of my father's mind and mine, there was this notion that I would follow in his footsteps with a career in law. He had intended me to attend one of the temples of law in England—one didn't need to be a graduate then to be a bar-at-law—but the war intervened,' said Mr Dey with a faraway look in his eyes. With the perils of war, it was decided that the young B.K. Dey would stay in Calcutta and pursue a post-graduate course at the Scottish Church College in Calcutta. It was around that time that the pandemonium struck. 'Singapore had perhaps been taken and there were rumours that the Japanese were about to overrun eastern

India. And though there wasn't a Jap to be seen on land or sky, there was widescale panic!' Schools and other educational institutions issued notices to the effect that they were closing down indefinitely for the safety of the students till such time as it was considered safe for them to return. B.K. Dey had been looking forward to representing his college at the inter-college debate at Nagpur along with Dilip Biswas, but with that notice, all was put to naught. That was 1941, and the young man though very homesick was smitten by wanderlust. Almost unintentionally, he found himself in Fort William signing up for an emergency commission as an officer of the armed forces. The selection commission had selected him for the navy but they did not know that the candidate knew nothing about swimming and was terrified of water. That, however, was not the explanation he gave, as he needled tactfully out of the situation he found himself in. He said, 'I feel you would be doing a grave injustice by putting me into any service other than the army.' Consequently, he was dubbed with the first pips, that made him Second Lieutenant, at the Artillery School at Deolali.

Time went by and having being posted first to a nonfighting formation in Quetta, he was subsequently moved to a fighting formation east of India, in the Arakans and Burma. He saw a lot of action while there but he is one of the few who saw the conception of the 'Battle of Boxes'. To put it in his words, '...the Japs had an unnerving strategy of allowing the enemy to advance and when they had done that, to circle round the back and cut off the retreat. This resulted in heavy losses but, probably borrowing ancient Roman war strategy, the allied forces formed boxes that held position till the objective was achieved. The Japanese were shot out of the sky and the battle was won.' The victorious troops were sent back to recuperate by the sea from Rangoon to Bombay. There, the war was declared over and there was rumour of the 3rd Light being demolished. At roughly the same time, Lala B.K. Dey who had become a Captain by then, was struck by an attack of malaria. It was also at that time, lying cooped up in a hospital bed being fed on bitter doses of Quinine that an advertisement in the newspaper caught his eye: 'Wartime vacancies for emergency commissioned officers in the Civil Services,' which included the Indian Financial Service. By this time, the pining for home had taken on the proportions of ethnic depression and B.K. Dey opted for the Police Service, then the least sought after occupation for the simple reason that it carried with it the single most important perquisite of being stationed in one's home province.

Then, directives were issued that the Service was being provincialized and that the pay scale would be nothing more than Rs. 450. This was a definite drop for Lala B.K. Dey who had become a Major by this time, drawing a monthly salary of Rs. 1,100 but the heartstrings of home tugged hard and when he was asked for his decision, Major B.K. Dey chose the Police.

'When I first joined the Police, everything was in a melting pot. I never had any formal training in policing and everything I learned was picked up through practical experience. I also owe a great deal to a constable whose English had to be heard to be believed but who was an absolute genius when it came to dealing with denizens of the underworld. I was among the first batch of the All India Police Service.'

His has been an outstanding career by any standards. On the present law and order crisis being faced globally, he says, '...any human being takes an instinctive dislike to any who is out there to curtail or to even monitor his activities and, in that sense, the Police faces an uphill task.'

When asked about how the lack of absolute autonomity influences adversely the functioning of the force, he replied:

'I don't think that autonomity has much to do with the functioning at all. If there is something that an officer thinks has to be done, he goes ahead and does it. Provided that is, if he is serving with total integrity and that he is committed to policing. Most of the time, it (autonomity) is used as a convenient subterfuge.'

'Would you say that there has been a decline ever since the British left, in the police force in the country?' I ask.

'The force has grown too fast in too short a time with the result that it has given very little time to every officer in the force to learn his job thoroughly. There was a time when a British officer had to report to his higher-ups, in detail, what the circumstances were that caused him to draw his baton. Today, crime has escalated so much that no policeman goes unarmed. There are new-fangled devices such as rubber bullets and water hoses that have become the permanent gear of the new-world cop.'

As I prepare to leave, after the lovely breakfast his daughter has served us, the grand old man reminisces once more.

'There is one thing I admire the British for. Even at a time when they were in the process of being ousted from a country to which they had come to prove the supremacy of their race, they were concerned for it. As I was preparing to leave the army for the police, my adjutant, a British officer, told me, 'if all of you leave the regiment like this, who is going to manage it when we are gone?' Such was their spirit.'

Lala B.K. Dey retired on 31st December 1978 as Director General of Police in Shillong. He is currently leading the retired life of an active man on his farm at Mawprem.

As I walked down the drive from that picturesque gabled house, the strong figure with a cane in one hand, waving good bye with the other, reminded me of the words my grandfather often said, 'An old soldier never dies…. he only fades away!'

Lala Saheb

Chet Bahadur Chettri

Narrated to Purnima Chettri

I left Nepal and came to Assam in 1954 at the age of 19 or 20 years to join the service as a sepoy in the Border Security Force. The Unit Headquarters of the Second Battalion was at Salonibari near Tezpur and the Subedar Major and many of the jawans were originally from the army.

Sometime in 1960, when I was travelling back by train, hardly had I alighted from the bogey when the Subedar Major came up to me and informed me that I was to report before the DIG BSF at Shillong, for duties as a 'Shahayak' for 15 days only. He briefed me that Lala Saheb was a short-tempered man and he would take no nonsense from anyone. And there I was apprehensive as ever. I reported my arrival at the DIG Headquarters, which was then inside the Cantonment Area.

Before this, I had served in several Border Out Posts along the Indo-Pakistan border, namely, Borsora, Baghli,

Maheshkhola to name a few. The Pakistanis used to tease us by saying that we were more like women, but very often, when it came to a face-off, we would pin them down in their bunkers.

And so I was plunged into this new task—nervous as hell. The officer who was present at the DIG's office directed me to go to DIG saheb's residence at Umsohsun, along with my bedroll and other personal belongings.

At Umsohsun, I was confronted by a tall, well-built person with a loud voice—it was Lala Saheb. He, at once, directed his other staff to show me to my living quarters. This was the beginning of my long and emotional tie to a person who many could not understand. Being the caretaker (Shahayak) of Sir, Sahab liked and loved me and I have remained with Sahab till date.

Lala Sahab was particular about his breakfast and the best available milk had to be served at the table. Being his Shahayak, I use to bring 3 litres of milk for the house from Maham Singh's dairy—Maham Singh was the brother-in-law of Sahab.

Very soon, Maham Singh presented one cow to Sahab, so that he could enjoy milk from his own cow. Besides my other duties, I would supervise the care and upkeep of the cow which was given to Sahab by his brother-in-law. It started giving around 14-15 litres of milk per day.

Sahab became more interested in keeping cows and he discussed this with his brother-in-law (Maham Singh) who suggested that he should start a farm.

And so at Mawprem, the dairy farm was started on land that belonged to Maham Singh's family. It was given the name of Lakyrsiew Dairy Farm—Lakyrsiew (Nayantara) is the youngest daughter of Sahab.

After starting the farm at Mawprem, Sahab started constructing his own house on land as he decided to stay and retire there.

I also decided to retire from service and stay with Sahab, and accordingly, I moved to Mawprem with my family.

Lakyrsiew Dairy Farm started growing in size and in around 2 or 3 years, there were 30 to 40 cows in the shed, and Sahab decided to build new sheds for the cows because it was getting congested. So, Sahab constructed a shed where more than 80 cows could be kept. We bought more animals from as far away places as Darjeeling.

Time was going by smoothly, and Sahab and I kept ourselves busy in the Farm except for the period when we lost almost 86 cows because of a deadly disease. We were left with only 12 animals at the end of it. This, however, did not stop Sahab from continuing with his dairy farm—he was an animal lover after all.

Sahab was ageing and he started getting his old age sickness. I used to pray daily to God for Sahab's good health.

But one day, he left me all alone. The bonding between Sahab and me was great. I till now miss my Sahab very much.

With Sahab's blessing, I am still taking care of the cows and staying on the farm, remembering Sahab.

Chet Bahadur Chettri with Lala Sahab at Mawprem

Acknowledgements

My gratitude to Shri D.D. Lapang for his excellent foreword. Bijon for his meticulous research, in this labour of love, of father's army and police days. Nayantara for sifting through trunkful of papers and photographs and for the gems she unearthed. Atiar Singh Dey for his unstinted support throughout the writing process. Larsing L.D. Sawyan for his generosity in making this edition happen—perfect and raring to go. Manoj Jalan for contributing some informative details and pictures of Kohima. Uncles, Aunts and Cousins: Jayobrata Chaudhuri, Mona Desai, Vaijayanti Bose, Monica Sen Saha, (late) Ajay Ray Chaudhary and Kalyani Chaudhuri for their advice, contributions and long distance calls borne patiently. Gauri Trivedi and Arjun Trivedi for the interesting and personal anecdotes of their childhood in Shillong with my parents. Renuka Chatterjee for her invaluable help and suggestions. All our well-wishers, friends and relatives for sharing their memories verbally, and some in beautifully expressed tributes that are part of this book. My father's great-grandchildren, who never met him but will now through this book—Gabriella Triambika, Rinzoa, Larshansing, Anabelle Ilarimai, Ariashisha, Inaara Lily and Amaara Rose—you all inspired me to tell you this story.

Thank you.

APPENDICES

Appendix A

Retd. in 1902

Verses addressed to

The Honourable H. J. S. Cotton,

Chief Commissioner of Assam, — 1897 – 190

On the eve of his departure from India.

Farewell ! Britannia's noble son,
Farewell undoubted friend of Ind,
Manfully thou hast done thy part,
Crossed though at times by adverse wind.

Dearest that book of thine shall be
Ever to every Indian heart ;
Dearest that speech for coolies made,
Frustrate though 'twas by crooked art.

Ruler impartial, all to thee
Shaheb or native, were the same ;
Culprits of whate'er race or creed,
Trembling they stood all at thy name.

Piteous was the convicts' lot
Ere thy benignant rule began ;
Scantily fed and overworked,
Largely they died in every den.

McCabe's report of ninety-six
Melted thy noble heart, and there
A revolution great soon came :
Convicts too now are objects of care.

Planters' oppression next thy heart,
Full of the milk of kindness true,
Led to befriend the coolie's cause,
And to secure his wages due ;

Labour and Emigration Act
Came out in nineteen hundred-one ;
Fresh is the mem'ry of the storm ;
Fresh, of what all thou then hadst done.

Science and Arts within the reach
Thou of the poor hast kindly brought ;
Graduates here had e'er in thee
Patron sincere and earnest got.

Vive Sir Cotton ! every where
Breathes here in Assam every heart ;
Farewell ! Britannia's noble son ;
Manfully thou hast done thy part.

Appendix B

CIRCA 1945: THE BEGINNING

During the Golden Jubilee celebrations of The Shillong Times 25 years ago, our Founder Editor Late Sudhindra Bhushan Chaudhuri recounted his early days as a journalist and what spurred him to launch the weekly. He penned down his overriding thoughts that went on to formulate his editoral policy that of nationalistic but supportive of the myriad hill tribes who were languishing in the back waters of undivided Assam. He clearly envisioned The Shillong Times to be a veritable meeting ground for goodwill and amity for peoples of the hills and the plains. As we celebrate our Platinum Jubilee, we reproduce excerpts from his personal account of what led to the birth of The Shillong Times

By SB Chaudhuri
Founder Editor :1945-1961

The Shillong Times was born fifty years ago, but the seed of it was sown a decade earlier when sixty years ago another English weekly was born under the editorship ofLala Bijoy Kumar Dey, the eminent lawyer of the Shillong Bar of those days.

The Shillong Mail was a precursor to *The Shillong Times* and I doubt if there would have been a *Shillong Times* without *TheMail* preceding it. *The Mail* provided a congenial field for the *Times* to germinate in the fullness of times and it equipped the founder editor of the *Times* with rudimentary lessons in journalism.

It was September 1934. A fairly tangible crowd of relatives of Lala Dey gathered at the Nepali Press atdistant Upper Mawprem to offer help in bringing out the first issue of *The Shillong Mail* and, uninvited and unnoticed, I too was among the crowd. With the passage of time I remained the only one who continued to come to the Press, probably because I was unemployed even after a year of graduation.

Gandhi in 1930. Mr Nag, the mentor of my Calcutta days used to narrate his day's experience of newspaper work at his desk and all this I listened to as if in a romantic stance. Nag probably noticed this influence on me and hence when after my final B.A examination it was time to bid goodbye, he asked me what vocation I would like to choose.

I looked vacant and at this -he himself added: whatever be your choice, it must not be journalism. (Such was the bleak prospect of this profession in those days of worldwide economic depression). But God willed otherwise.

My association with the Mail ended with my joining the United Press of India (UPI), the now - defunct nationalist news agency - first as Correspondent in Shillong and then as Assistant Editor at its head office in Calcutta. When I was next transferred to Bombay I refused to move, since I did not like to lose my link with durjointfamily in Shillongand more importantly my interest in tribal affairs which I had imbibed during my years in The Shillong Mail. I came

the weekly in addition to their assignment, but after about six months when prospects of the weekly as a financial proposition was already fairly evident, the ABP-HS retracted on the plea that the policies of the weekly and the two dailies might clash and so offered as acompromise that I hand over ownership of The Shillong Times to AnandabazarPatrika Ltd. on the assurance that I continue as its Editor on behalf of the ABP Ltd. I did not agree and gave up the ABP-HS assignment to devote full time to my own publication. The Shillong Times was started with the primary object of serving tribal cause and interests despite tremendous odds.

Adequate facilities for smooth production of the paper were still lacking: of course, a power -driven treadle machine was not available. in contrast with a hand machine (discarded by

was the administrative headquarters of Assam. One reason for this lapse obviously was that there were no Congress unit in the entire hills belt to receive the Rashrapati (as the Congress President was then called.) Sporadic attempts were of course, made by different groups of political workers, mostly from Sylhet (which although part of Assam administratively was under Bengal Provincial Congress Committee) to establish Congress units in Shillong but they had no access to the Assam Provincial Congress Committee headquarters in Guwahati.

In contrast, the hills tribals themselves were already showing signs of coming under the influence of the national upsurge throughout the country as would be evident from the fact that groups of tribals came to greet Nehru with gifts of fruits and flowers as

was much later that it became almost a passion with Nehru himself in the early post - independence years to talk ad nauseum about development of the hills tribes "according to their own tradition and genius." This apt Nehruvian expression has become almost a bye-word now in Congress parlance and policy- making. Verrier Elwin's now famous "philosophy"for NEF A was the product of this vision of Jawaharlal Nehru who wrote an appropriate foreword for Elwin' s book. Nehru was now more than ready to makes amends for skipping the hills during his first Assam tour as the Congress President.

The Shillong Times soon became extremely popular but ironically, this fact itself created the third problem for me - apathy, if not antipathy, of the government of the day towards The Shillong Times. The paper's pronouncedly pro-tribal policy did not quite fit in with the government's policy in this regard. At one stage the relationship became so hardened that the then

then for another six months to give up the chase ultimately. No wonder when the weekly was converted into a daily forthefirst time in its tenth year the reckless adventure was destined for failure. The Times was back to its weekly periodicity. After about another five years it was time for me to "abdicate" and leave Shillong out of my own volition (which is a different story). By now the hills tribes of this region had already come to their own - politically and in every other respect and were perceptibly approaching a new dawn with self-rule conceded for the newly-carved hill states for different well-knit hill tribal groups. With my imminent departure, there was now a proposal discussed that the All-Party Hills Leaders Conference which led the Hills State Movement to fruition should take over The Shillong Times to make it the official mouthpiece of this unified tribal leadership. For this purpose, the then Secretary of the APHLC the late-lamented Stanley Nichols Roy visited passage of time I remained the only one who continued to come to the Press, probably because I was unemployed even after a year of graduation.

All the rest dropped out, being otherwise employed. The entire burden of the paper (excepting leader-writing and financing) fell on me. This labour of love, which I regard as my apprenticeship, I have never regretted since it stood me in good stead in later years Above all, it provided me a real insight as much into the rudimentaries of the working of a mofussil newspaper as into the money facets of the local tribal life and society. The fruitful association would not have been possible without an interest in the work on the love for the profession.

This love was inculcated in me probably because of my earlier association with a Calcutta journalist, the late Bhabesh Chandra Nag (also of Sylhet) who was a: boarder of the same messing establishment when I came to Calcutta for my under-graduate studies after being rusticated from the M C College for participation in the first Civil Disobedience Movement of Mahatma link with ourjointfamily in Shillongand more importantly my interest in tribal affairs which I had imbibed during my years in The Shillong Mail. I came back to Shillong but this time with the additional charge of representing the AnandabazarPatrika and Hindustan Standard.

Even as I was declining the UPI post, was harbouring the idea of starting a paper of my own - a legacy of my Shillong Mail experience. (By the way, the Mail had by then ceased publication). The difficulty was that publication of a newspaper in those days required prior clearance from New Delhi because of strict enforcement of the Newsprint Control Orders during the War years. Luckily, however, the then Director ofInformation and Publicity, Mr T.T.S. Hailey, a young British I.C.S. officer took kindly on me and strongly recommended my application, but even then the permission took eight months to come. Instantly I proceeded to bring out the first issue without any prior elaborate planning or much fanfare. The ABP-HS agreed to allow me to run duction of the paper were still lacking: of course, a power -driven treadle machine was not available, in contrast with a hand-machine (discarded by the Government Press) on which The Shillong Mail had to depend a decade earlier. The more formidable deterrent was the lack of adequate readership for this political weekly since political consciousness had not yet dawned on the tribal communities to the extent necessary for sustenance of paper committed to such an obscure cause. The colonial rulers had their own reasons to isolate the tribes from the mainstream of Indian life, but there was none whatsoever for the National leadership not to come closer to tribal life even as late as the late thirties and early forties.

Jawharlal Nehru, for instance, came to visit Assam (then comprising the entire north-eastern region) for the first time on a ten-day tour covering about all the plains districts and sub-divisional headquarters, but not a single hill-station was included in his itinerary, not even Shillong which tional upsurge throughout the country as would be evident from the fact that groups of tribals came to greet Nehru with gifts of fruits and flowers as the special train carrying him passed through the hill section of the then Assam Bengal Railway from Lumding to Silchar. My esteemed friend the late Akhil Chandra Bhattacharyya of the Amrita Bazar Patrika and I were the two lone journalists accompanying Jawaharlal on this tour to witness this spontaneous love and affection on the part of the tribals of the Mikir and North Cachar Hills for a national leader. I was convinced that an artificial barrier existed between the hills tribes and the rest of the country, for which geography can only partly be held responsible.

Psychological factors were the more disturbing agents and therefore when I decided to start a paper of my own in later years the idea came to me instantly to pledge the paper to this virgin field of working to build a bridge and initiating a breakthrough in this unexplored area of national service. It edly pro-tribal policy did not quite fit in with the government's policy in this regard. At one stage the relationship became so hardened that the then Chief Minister, the late Bishnu Ram Medhi ordered my expulsion from Assam. When I learnt of it much later from a source having access to the secret Secretariatfile it was my eternal regret that the orderwas not executed, thus preventing my becoming a sort of a martyr!What happened was that Mr Suresh Chandra Bhattacharyya had about that time taken over as the first Assamese Director ofInformation and Publicity and he did not quite relish the prospect of a severe controversy in the Press over this governmental action. He was obviously loathe to lose his reputation as a working journalist oflong standing asa successful Editor-ProprietorofThe Rangoon Mail.

The Rangoon Mail and The Shillong Mail were on each other's mailing lists and I was personally known to him from my Shillong Mail days. Bhattacharyya asked for three months to "watch"how the paper fared and [illegible] tribal leadership. For this purpose, the then Secretary of the APHLC the late-lamented Stanley Nichols Roy visited my office in Laitumkhrah several times but the deal could not be finalised despite several meetings of the plenary body ofthe APHLC.

On my part I was in a hurry and could not prolong the negotiation. Meanwhile, myesteemed mend, the late Mr ParswaNath Chaudhuri came forward to run the paper. I was satisfied that the policy of the paper would not suffer any dilution under his care and its tradition would be scrupulously maintained.

Let, The Shillong Times continue to serve the people of these hills and remain a shining symbol of Hills-Plains amity and fraternity of mutual love and friendship on the basis of the salutary principle of live and let live to make these hills once again the' 'abode of peace"as it has been until the very recent past —an oasis in the midst of engulfing turmoil and conflict' all around.

THOSE TUMULTUOUS 30 YEARS

■CONTINUED FROM P-I

We had no reason to oblige them since factually our news report was correct. For over a week, neither the staff could enter the office nor *The Shillong Times* could be circulated. I declined to seek police assistance, since, in my opinion, journalists must not be seen surviving under police protection. Once again, the saner section of citizens in Tura took the initiative for a possible rapprochement. We drove down to Tura where in a desolate place that night we sat with the agitated youths, heard their side of the story and placed ours before them. Although there was no formal thaw, we reopened our office the next morning without any hitch.

Of the high points of this journey of 30 years, one has to be the Government of India's enlistment of *The Shillong Times* as one of top regional dailies of the country. We began to get invited to 'national' media-related events and were part of the select band of journalists accompanying the Prime Minister abroad. One was privileged to be part of Atal Bihari Vajpayee's historic tour of Islamabad for a summit with Gen Parvez Musharraf and subsequently the several tours Manmohan Singh undertook, be it the summit with President George W. Bush at White House or with British Prime Minister Tony Blair at 10 Downing Street. It was an experience of a lifetime.

This story will remain incomplete without a mention of the personal glory bestowed on me by the Government of India by way of Padma Sri award in journalism. In my considered view, it was a veritable recognition for *The Shillong Times* and not me per se. I believe this award belongs to the Founder Editor Sudhindra Bhusan Chaudhuri, the doyen of journalism in the Northeast. As my mentor and a lifetime inspiration, he instilled in me the true spirit of journalism. I owe the award to him.

In 2005, most unexpectedly and amidst a big family tragedy (my elder brother and MLA Ardhendu Chaudhuri died in a helicopter crash), I had to plunge myself into the whirlpool of politics. As an Independent MLA, pursuing the people's cause helped performing the dual role of Editor and a legislator for three years. But never did I use the daily to advance the cause of politics nor did I use my new authority to promote the interest of the newspaper. In 2008, when I was re-elected to the Assembly and joined the Cabinet, dramatically my pursuit and priority changed. For a hard-nosed journalist, it is always a delight to open the official files and ferret out information worthy of news. And now, as a minister, it was my avowed duty to keep things under the wraps. I must say with legitimate pride that I did not betray that trust.

I consider myself extremely privileged to have had a small hand in shaping *The Shillong Times* to become a credible public platform for the citizens to freely air their aspirations and grievances alike. That *The Shillong Times*, under the able care of my worthy successor Patricia Mukhim, continues to be a free-thinking daily is extremely gratifying. I am sanguine that by the time the daily reaches its centenary, it will scale newer peaks as an unflinching custodian of public trust and a vehicle for achieving the collective aspirations of the people. Long live *The Shillong Times*!

A journey I did not choose

■CONTINUED FROM P-I

A neighbour said she saw two young men hurling the petrol bomb and rushing off on a motor cycle. Their faces were masked. Till date police have not been able to arrest anyone. The incident left behind its own scars but not deep enough to deter the journalist in me from ignoring my inner voice.

Another incident that left deep psychological scars was when in December 2018 the publisher, Ms Shobha Chaudhuri and I were hauled up for contempt of court. *The Shillong Times* had published a story captioned, "When judges judge for themselves", which pertained to retirement benefits for judges and which mentioned among other things entitlements such a mobile phone costing Rs 80,000 and mobile phone bills to the extent of Rs 10,000 to be payable not only to judges but to their dependents as well. At the first hearing both the publisher and I tendered our unconditional apology. But the learned Judge summarily rejected the apology on the plea that our body language did not convey absolute contrition. The Judge who was also the complainant in the same case asked me sternly, "What's your qualification?" When I informed the Court of my degrees I was told, "You are not qualified to be a newspaper editor." That was meant to deliver a body blow to my self esteem and to humiliate me and the publisher in an open court. Later while sharing this malady we were told, "Judges reserve the right to say anything they choose to." "But isn't that verbal abuse?" I asked. They had no answer.

The ordeal of having to appear almost every week before the same judge and to be subjected to such humiliation was traumatizing. It was then I realized how difficult it is to find justice when a judge has already decided that you are guilty and has everything is arraigned against you. We could not also understand why the judge made personal comments that were not related to the case.

After the winter vacation the Court reopened and we attended more hearings. Finally, on March 8, 2019 the divisional bench of the Meghalaya High Court ruled that we were guilty of contempt and asked us to sit in a corner of the court till it's rising. We were slapped with a fine of Rs two lakh each to be deposited within March 15, 2019. This fine was unprecedented since no court has ever penalised any contemnor with an amount exceeding Rs 2000. We felt that the judgment was inherently flawed and prejudiced and appealed to the Supreme Court. On March 15, the Meghalaya High Court order was stayed. The case is now pending with the Supreme Court and we are awaiting the final judgment.

Here we must acknowledge the unstinted support of the Editors' Guild of India which has upheld our right to Freedom of Expression. Local rights groups too stood by us solidly during our hour of trial in the Meghalaya High Court. Further the Press Council of India too has stepped in to file a separate petition in the Supreme Court to challenge the Meghalaya High Court judgment in our case.

The above are just a few instances of the travails of pursuing journalism in a small town where everyone knows everyone else and where you are expected to brush under the carpet any misdemeanor committed by people in your circle of acquaintances. Beyond a point you rise above the flotsam and just do your duty. To the credit of *The Shillong Times* and its management, they have remained unstintingly committed to the highest ideals of free and fair journalism. And that perhaps is the reason why the newspaper is both loved and hated but there is none that is indifferent to it.

In the 75th year of this historic newspaper that has experienced many ups and downs, we hope to see readers engage with us better and also share their concerns, critiques and their inspirational thoughts with us. We value readers' feedback on how to improve our services to the people of this state, the country and the world. I wish to thank all our readers, and especially those that have enriched our editorial pages as regular contributors. You are the anchor on which *The Shillong Times* rests. What would our editorial page be without the letters that range from the esoteric and metaphysical to the concerns of ordinary folks; from the political to the social; from the spiritual to the temporal! Reading these letters and editing them has always been a fulfilling task as it gives us insights into what's ailing our democracy and governance.

We raise a toast to *The Shillong Times* and to all those readers who help us to redefine good journalism! We wish even those, who for reasons best known to themselves, choose to ban our paper from entering their territories for it takes all kinds to make the world. And variety is what keeps journalism interesting! As we proceed to the next level of our journey we will have to prepare for the challenges ahead. With AI taking the world of humans by storm, news-gathering and editing will require new and more dynamic talent which the younger generation of media students will have to arm themselves with. But we are sure they will succeed better and keep the flag flying. At *The Shillong Times* we have always given space to younger, creative and innovative talent and they have never let us down. We hope this newspaper will see that creative team taking it to the next level and the next……

Appendix C

28th November 1941.

Lala Bimalendu K. Dey was a student of this School and College for about twelve years. He graduated with Honours in Economics from this College in 1941.

He has had a uniformly bright career obtaining First Grade in the Senior Cambridge Examination 1936. He comes of a respectable Shillong family and, so far as I know, bears a good moral character.

He was a brilliant and witty speaker of the Debating Society, played most outdoor games well and was generally reliable. I think he will prove to be a competent worker in whatever sphere of life he adopts and I can with confidence recommend him to employers.

Signed.

J. I. O'Leary,
Principal.

Appendix D

Delhi 7041/35.

No. 6872/1887/Org.9(c)(i),
General Headquarters,
Adjutant General's Branch,
New Delhi, the 28 March'47.

To

Capt. L.B. Kumar Dey, R.I.A.,
No. 3 Field Regt., R.I.A.,
Rawalpindi.

APPOINTMENT OF "WAR SERVICE" CANDIDATES TO THE NEW ALL INDIA POLICE SERVICE.

1. Government of India, Home Department letter No. 45/8/46-Ests (R) dated the 22nd March '47 is forwarded for immediate action.

2. Please acknowledge receipt immediately of this Home Department letter and (on a separate sheet of paper) furnish the following particulars.

1. Pers.No.	2. Rank	3. Name	4. Initials	5. Unit	6. Age/Service Gp. & Code letters.	7. Whether candidate for a Reg. or S.S. Commission.

3. Please note that you are now only being asked whether or not you accept the offer made by the Home Department, Government of India of an appointment in the All India Police Service.

4. The date, time and place of medical examination will be communicated later. This medical examination will as far as possible, be held at the Provincial Headquarters nearest to your station.

5. No (NO) action will be taken at this stage for your release from Army Service which will be dealt with by this Headquarters in due course as the release is dependent on your being passed medically fit.

[illegible signature]
Major
for Adjutant General in India.

Copy to (Less enclosure)

O.C., No. 3 Field Regt., R.I.A.,
Rawalpindi.

Defence Deptt. (D-6) Mr. R.N. Vasudeva for information. Your U.O. No. 1937-A/D-6 dated 25 March '47 refers.

Home Department Mr. Abdullah J[illegible] for information.

Org. 8(a).

Appendix E

No. VI 23011/5/77-GPAIII
Government of India/Bharat Sarkar
Ministry of Home Affairs/Grih Mantralaya

New Delhi, the, May, 1977
Vais, 1899

Corrigendum

In notification No. VI 23011/5/77-GPAIII dated the 5th May 1977 issued by the Ministry of Home Affairs the date of appointments of Shri R.K. Gupta Inspector General of Police West Bengal Shri N.S. Saksena Director General Central Reserve Police Force and Shri Lala B.K. Dey Director of Civil Defence and Commandant General Home Guards as Honorary Police Aide-De-Camp to the President may be read as 11th February 1977 instead of 12th February 1977 mentioned therein.

(C.S. Chadha)
Deputy Secretary to the Govt. of India.

No. VI 23011/5/77 GPA III

New Delhi, 110001, the, May 1977
Vais. 1899

Copy forwarded for information to the:- 11 MAY 1977

(1) Military Secretary to the President New Delhi.
(2) Secretary to the Prime Minister New Delhi.
(3) Cabinet Sectt. New Delhi.
(4) Chief Secretary to the Govt. of West Bengal/Assam
(5) Shri R.K. Gupta Inspector General of Police West Bengal.
(6) Shri. N.S. Saksena Director General Central Reserve Police Force, New Delhi.
(7) Shri Lala B.K. Dey Inspector General of Police Assam Gauhati.

(C.S. Chadha)
Deputy Secretary to the Govt. of India.

Appendix F

Copy of Letter.No.HPL.117/55/181, dated the 27th May, 1955 from Joint Secretary to the Governmentof Assam to the Inspector General of Police, Assam, Shillong.

Referance:- Your Memo.No.F-XXII/45/256 dated 23-6-54.

I am directed to convey the sanction of the Governor of Assam to the grant of a special pay of Rs.200/- P.M. (Rupees two hundred only) to Shri Lala Bimalendu Kumar Dey, I.P.S., Superintendent of Police, Sibsagar, for holding the post of special Superintendent of Police for Border Security duties, during the period 25th March 1950 to the 10th January, 1951.

The expenditure is debitable to the head "29-Police-G-C.I.D. - B.S.F." in the current year's budget.

....

Memo.No.HPL.117/55/181-A. Dated Shillong, the May, 1955.

Copy forwarded to -

(1) Finance (E) Department with 2 spare copies for favour of communication to the Accountant General, Assam. The sanction has been communicated with the concurrence of the Finance Department vide their U/O No.FE/1143/55 dated 26-4-55.

(2) Shri Lal Bimalendu Kumar Dey, I.P.S., S.P., Sibsagar.

(3) Shri V.N.Singh, I.A. & A.S.,Accountant General, Assam,

By order of the Governor of Assam,

Sd/- D.Das,

Joint Secretary to the Govt. of Assam.

.....

Memo.No.F/XXII/45/341. Dated Shillong, the June, 1955.

Forwarded to Shri Lala Bimalendu Kumar Dey, I.P.S., Superintendent of Police, Sibsagar for information.

Assistant Inspector General of Police,
Assam.

KD/10/6.

....

Appendix G

FIELD MARSHAL SIR WILLIAM SLIM.
"DEFEAT INTO VICTORY"

a destroyer flotilla, and later an aircraft carrier with the quick-thinking, instant decisions and direct control of men that such tasks call for, were the finest possible training for tactical command. His period as Chief of Combined Operations gave him an insight into the organization and working of the other two Services that was of tremendous value to him; but the tactical planning of combined operations involves, more than any other, attention to and concentration on detail, in contrast to the broader, long-term considerations that are the province of a supreme commander. It was as a member of the Chiefs of Staffs Committee for Combined Operations, where he came into contact with the wider direction of the war as a whole, that he served his apprenticeship for supreme command.

His comparative youth—he was ten years younger than I and twenty years younger than Stilwell—was something of a stimulant to most of us, and certainly to our troops. There may have been a few in the Navy, where they are more stripe conscious, who found it hard to forget that they were admirals when he was a commander, but in the Army we are more tolerant in these matters. We are too accustomed to the vagaries of acting and temporary rank. My substantive rank when I became Army Commander was still Colonel, but I do not think that bothered anyone very much. From the very start, no one could fail to like the Supreme Commander—even Stilwell, in a picturesque phrase, once admitted that to me—and his quick brain, backed by a remarkable memory and tireless vitality, enabled him to grasp the intricacies of the whole vast organization of which he was the head. He came more and more to concentrate on essentials and to look farther ahead, until he was in every sense a real supreme commander.

I found Supreme Headquarters a fascinating place to wander through. It was full of interesting people, not least persuasive young men interested in selling short cuts to victory, of which they held the rights of way. These 'racketeers', as I called them, were of two kinds, those whose acquaintance with war was confined to large non-fighting staffs where they had had time and opportunity to develop their theories, and tough, cheerful fellows who might be first-class landed on a beach at night with orders to scupper a sentry-post, but whose experience was about the range of a tommy-gun. I liked talking to them and they were

Appendix H

Salute to an old soldier

By B. S. Baber
Retd. Director General of Police

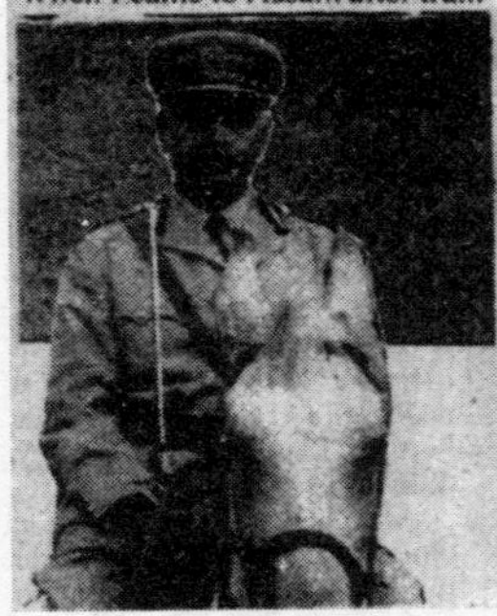

LALA B.K. DEY -- A TRIBUTE

When I came to Assam after training at the Central Police Academy as an IPS officer in 1956, I met Lala Bimalendu Kumar Dey who was then Supdt of Police Sibsagar Jorhat. In him I found all the good qualities which we were told are required to be a good and successful Police officer such as Personal leadership and integrity to lead from the front looking after the welfare of the forces and the junior officers. I found all these qualities in abundance in Dey; a handsome, well built popular officer, respected and loved by people and police force.

In November 1956 at the height of the Naga insurgency; DIG Mr.H. Hussain, DC Mr. Vaghariwalla ICS Lala Dey and myself a young A.S.P. while attending a musical confernce in the evening at Jorhat had to go to a Border under attack and had to spend whole night under firing. The courage inspired by personal leadership by Dey greatly encouraged me in the rest of my career in Police.

In 1966 at Silchar during a popular agitation, Dey, then as D.I.G. along with the Commissioner, Deputy Commissioner, the Supdt of Police was commanding the Distt Police and C.R.P.F. contingent. Due to some misunderstanding CRPF opened fire killing about 13 persons. Though Dey had not ordered the firing; he took all responsibility on his broad shoulders though he was not responsible.

When I was DIG in IGP office, his advice was office, his advice was to see the men are not starved and also to exercise all the powers of the IGP but keep him informed. He was a leader who could delegate the authority to his officers in the interest of force.

In his death on July 10 last Assam Police has lost an inspiring leader whom Police respected and trusted. My salute to the departed leader on the day of shradh.